smack
my
pitch
up!

smack
my
pitch
up!

business writing success

ANDREAS LOIZOU

urbanepublications.com

First published in Great Britain in 2015 by Urbane Publications Ltd
Suite 3, Brown Europe House, 33/34 Gleamingwood Drive,
Chatham, Kent ME5 8RZ
Copyright © Andreas Loizou, 2015

A CIP catalogue record for this book is available from the British Library.

ISBN 978-1-910692-45-5
EPUB 978-1-910692-46-2
KINDLE 978-1-910692-47-9

Design and Typeset by Julie Martin
Cover by Julie Martin
Printed and bound by CPI Group (UK) Ltd, Croydon, CR0 4YY

urbanepublications.com

To my sisters
Kathy, Christie and Nicolette -
with love and gratitude

foreword
well done, you!

Smack my pitch up! A controversial title for a book, I'm sure you'll agree. Many congratulations for choosing something a bit risky.

The alternative titles included drivel like *Better Written Communication for Executives.* I'm sure we even threw around the horrible word *solutioneering.* But I wanted something that really stood out, really grabbed your attention and really made you think. It's worked, hasn't it?

I've never believed in books that promise to change your life in a day. You know the ones – *The Seven Minute MBA* and *Fake It Till You Make It (A Surgeon's Guide).* But here I am, telling you that I'll change your writing forever in just over 200 pages. It sounds like a big task, but it's completely feasible.

Why? As soon as you turn these pages, you'll learn how.

I promise.

contents

part 2

writing is an emotional business   53

part 3

Structure 97

part 4

Crafting Your Style 133

part 5

Words, words, words

part 6

Happy Endings 183

introduction

Let me tell you what you'll gain from being a better writer.

You'll be **more successful**, because business writing helps you achieve your objectives. Use these new skills to inspire millions, or stop the idiots in accounts from photocopying their privates.

You'll **save time**. Great writing comes from good planning, and good planning leads to a smarter use of time. You're not just saving your own time – people love writing they can understand immediately.

You'll **get noticed**. And for the right reasons. Most business writing is abstract and cold. Business writers who connect with other humans are rare, so people whose writing shows empathy and charisma are admired. The extra work you put in now will mean you stand out from the crowd.

You'll **be happier**. I'm not saying that great business writing skills leads to fame, fortune and true love. But it's worth a try, right?

You'll receive vital advice on how to attract readers and, once they're completely in your thrall, turn them into loyal followers. Your confidence will grow as you learn how to structure and plan your writing. You'll get messages across quickly. And you'll do it with style.

This book contains a handful of useful exercises. Do them.

Who wants to be more successful, save time, get noticed and be happier? That's right. Everyone!

Now read on…

part one

the reader comes first

it's all about the reader

This book is structured both for those who want to eat their meal in one sitting, and for those who prefer to graze. You can read it from cover to cover, because each module builds on what's gone before. But you'll be equally happy diving in to the bits that most interest you. We all learn in different ways.

See what I did there? I put you – the reader – first. Far too many business people moan that their readers don't 'get' what they're writing about. That's like a musician blaming his audience for his instrument being out of tune. If a reader doesn't respond to your writing, it's your fault.

Humans have always judged by first impressions. Our ancestors had to make rapid decisions about the person walking towards their cave carrying a club in his hairy hand. Was he friend or foe, diner or dinner?

These days, of course, we don't have to worry about

being attacked by hostile tribes.[1] But we still assess people primarily on whether they can influence us through their power, empathy or a mixture of the two.

It's a myth that influencers are born. They're made. Influencing is a skill (like learning a second language) and not part of your genetic make-up (like being exceptionally good-looking).

You are just like your readers. Busy. And you'll ignore anything that's incoherent or irrelevant. You'd rather eat your own eyes than struggle through another pompous, patronising and confusing email. And you judge people by how well – or how badly – they communicate with you.

Sadly, too much business writing is concerned with showing off the power of the writer. Poorly structured, packed with jargon and full of redundant words, it deflates rather than inspires. But charismatic writers are different. They know how to get the reader on their side. And a reader who's on your side will keep turning the page.

---

1   Doesn't apply to those of you in Investment Banks

feelings, actions, beliefs

Writers want to change their reader's Feelings, Actions or Beliefs (acronym junkies will be ecstatic to know we're shortening this to **FAB**). One really good way to understand the difference between feelings, actions and beliefs is to study adverts

Some adverts are designed to change how you *feel*. So, for example, a new car makes you want to tear up the countryside because you're now an empowered adventurer. Or the divine taste of that chocolate means you feel relaxed and stress free.

Other adverts want you to *act*. They want you to *switch* accounts, *visit* a craft fair or *come in and talk to us* about your investments. The most important act that companies want us to do is *buy*.

What about *beliefs*? Estate agents are trying to change what we think when they describe a house as *individualistic* rather than *odd-shaped*. Calling the fifteen-minute run to the nearest station *a pleasant stroll* is another belief-changer.

To make change happen, you need to know how to influence the reader. Always keep the FAB in mind as you write. Every word should influence what the reader feels, acts or believes. Don't write another word until you know what you want to change.

learning from
the professional
influencers

All adverts are meant to influence the reader. Everything
– from a multi million pound press campaign to a three
line listing on Gumtree – aims to influence FAB.

Certain words change how you feel, change how you
act, or change what you believe.

To see influence in action, take a look at this piece by
Coca-Cola on their Ekocycle clothing range. (Ekocycle is
where 'fashion and recycling collide.' Apparently.)

This luxurious and innovative brand, which has collaborated with adidas and Misfit, aims to push the boundaries on more sustainable fashion and design. By identifying everyday household items, including plastic bottoles and aluminium cans, and recycling them into valuable goods, EKOCYCLE challenges preconceived notions of products made from recycled materials.

Check out the range here: http://www.haroods.com/brand/ekocycle

Did you know? The idea for EKOCYCLE was born after will.i.am was inspired to turn waste from a Black Eyed Peas gig into recycled sought-after objects.

"Sustainability is at the heart of The Coca-Cola Company and we are always looking at innovative ideas that link the vision of sustainability with our packaging, and encourage its collection and recycling in order to extend the valuable lifecycle of this resource." **Bea Perez, Vice President and Chief Sustainability Officer, The Coca-Cola Company**

These two short paragraphs work hard for Coca-Cola. It seems like a fairly relaxed piece of marketing, but there's a lot going on. Remember, someone well paid and highly skilled is trying to change your FAB. What do you notice?

Here are some of the points I jotted down. You may well have different ideas. That's entirely fine, since every reader is different…and is influenced differently.

figure 1 How the Ad Influences my Feelings, Actions and Beliefs

Feelings

- Coca-cola is a nice company that cares about the environment, rather than a polluter
- If I buy these clothes my lifestyle will improve
- Coke is a premium product

Actions

- Recycle more packaging
- Buy these clothes
- Buy more Coke

Beliefs

- These clothes are luxurious, innovative, fashionable and good for the environment
- Consequently, Coke is luxurious, innovative, fashionable and good for the environment

Good writers know readers have preconceived ideas about a particular brand. They'll still work flat out to change the reader's feelings, actions and beliefs. To be an influential writer know your FAB.

readers demand useful, interesting or enjoyable

4

The reader is the most important person in the writing process. It's not about you, it's about them.

You have to give people at least one reason to start reading. The stronger the reason – and the more reasons you give – the greater the probability they will stick with you. If your writing doesn't strike readers as Useful or Interesting or Enjoyable, then forget it. Or – better still – revise it. [2]

Useful writing has a practical, immediate purpose. Your message offers the reader an immediate benefit – there are free croissants on the fifth floor, there are angry investors with burning torches outside the building.

---

2   Sorry, acronym junkies, I'm not going to start using UIE.

figure 2   Useful Writing

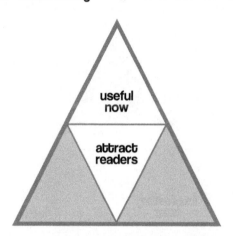

When your pipes burst, you don't care about beautiful design and witty *bon mots* in the advert. The plumber's contact details are enough to guarantee a high level of usefulness. Enjoyable and interesting aren't important when your home is flooding.

Interesting writing makes the reader curious. The message is mentally filed (or saved to your computer) because it will have a value in the future. The map telling you how to get to next week's conference in Nicosia is interesting, as is the forecasted demand for jetpacks in 2030.

figure 3 Interesting Writing

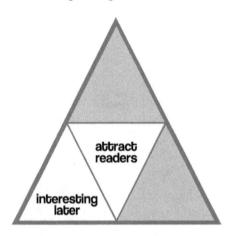

I often clip online articles with Evernote and Apple Reader. A feature on my favourite crime writers is not immediately useful, but I know I'll read it later before going to a bookshop.

Enjoyable writing gives pleasure to the reader. It could be an article that raises a smile, or includes fresh examples that keep the reader hooked. This is the category that suffers the most in business writing, but it's also one that you can improve very easily.

You'll know your business writing is enjoyable when people tell you *I loved the analogies you used to explain futures and options*. Or even, simply, *for the first time in my life I actually read your whole email.* Your expenses memo won't win the Nobel Prize for Literature, but you can make it clear and punchy and even try a joke.

figure 4   Enjoyable Writing

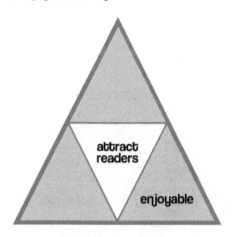

All readers are time sensitive, so you have to convince them your writing scores high in at least one segment of the triangle. In an ideal world, of course, you would show more than one of these attributes. If you can make your writing both interesting and enjoyable you're on to a winner.

The Holy Grail is to score in all three segments. It can be done, but it needs skill and hard work. And even the greatest writers in the world find it impossible to continually achieve all three of these objectives.

Don't knock yourself out about this. As long as you clearly show one attribute you'll secure readers.

figure 5 Useful, Interesting and Enjoyable Writing

Writing does not guarantee communication. We've all got emails we've never opened and texts we've never read. Successful communication only occurs when the reader engages with your words.

As you write and as you plan, continually check that your work is useful, interesting or enjoyable. This is the best way to give the reader reasons to choose your writing.

Take whatever you're reading now – an historical novel, a fashion website, an email from a friend – and map it to the triangle waiting for you at:
www.smackpitch.com/triangle.

how hot is your reader?

Let's think more about making the initial connection with our potential readers. My method – based on hours hanging around in bookshops – uses a thermometer to gauge their eagerness.

- A *cold reader* is a person walking past a bookshop.

- A *warm reader* is sipping a caramel latte in the bookshop's coffee bar while browsing through a large pile of books.

- And a *hot reader* is at the till point with their selection and an eager expression.

I'll show you how this works in business with the example of Augusto Astudillo, a corporate financier based in Madrid. Something of a Latin smoothie, Augusto has built strong relationships with clients in glamorous locations such as New York, Buenos Aires and Lisbon.

Augusto once sent an introductory email to the Chief Financial Officer of a company based in Panama City. I can't remember why Augusto didn't want to travel out there, but it was either the rainy season (January to June) or the mosquito season (July to December).

The CFO began as an extremely cold reader of Augusto's first email. She sent a fairly curt reply – *we have no need for new financing* – and filed his email with those from all the other banks. But a few weeks later, her MD asked her what banks were currently active in Panama. She remembered Augusto's first email, and wrote for some more details about his bank.

Augusto skilfully matched his writing to the CFO's temperature. She was thawing, so he sent materials that would increase her knowledge of the bank and build up trust between them. This stage is much more about brand awareness than pushing products.

At the end of the next quarter the MD asked her to look into different ways to finance an acquisition. She became warmer, questioning Augusto about the pros and cons of bond issues, bank debt and equity placements. Augusto, ever alert to opportunity, wrote longer answers. He didn't send precise details of deals because they would have been ignored during the warm stage.

His potential client became increasingly receptive to his emails and asked more involved questions about the different financial products in Augusto's armoury. Things heated up when the MD told her the company had decided on a bank loan. Augusto sent her a comprehensive analysis of how much money could be raised and in what currencies. He provided intricate details about yields, fees, timescales and maturities.

Augusto knew he wouldn't get to the hot stage unless he'd written to the CFO during the cold and warm stages. His groundwork ensured he was in the client's mind when they needed to make a decision. With the relationship established, Augusto is now seen as a trusted advisor rather than a salesman.

What do we learn from Augusto? Influence isn't always achieved instantly, so be prepared to play the long game with your writing. Knowing the temperature of your reader is essential if you want your communication to build rapport.

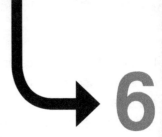

the art of introduction

It's wrong to believe that cold readers get too many emails. The real problem is that they get too many emails that don't give them a reason to carry on with the conversation.

Someone receiving your introductory email or LinkedIn request is a cold reader. They don't know who you are, so your job is to warm them up.

What should you do? It's far better to spend time crafting one fantastic, super-targeted email than swamping the world with a million sloppy mails. Think sniper, not shotgun blast. And don't get overly sensitive about being rejected or ignored. There are plenty of people out there who will want to read your message.

You can only consider an email successful if it's made the recipient feel, act or think differently. Your email must change the recipient's feelings (*I'm really happy with my bank*), actions (*I've changed to another bank*) or beliefs (*wow, my bank sucks*).

The first paragraph is often where we feel most blocked. A weak intro is the written equivalent of the dead-fish handshake. It's a hesitant, awkward start to any communication, reminiscent of those people who ring you up and say *it's only me.* Their very first words put them at a disadvantage.

Here's one tip I normally keep secret but am happy to share with you. I sometimes warm up my writing muscles by finding a really good introduction written by someone else. Then I copy the first two sentences out in long hand, crossing out some words and replacing them with words that reflect my own subject matter. So, *manipulative* becomes *charismatic, yesterday* becomes *last year, profit* becomes *loss* and *boss* becomes *arrogant little s**t.*

We unconsciously imitate people's skills all the time in many other areas, but the fear of being labelled a plagiarist holds us back when it comes to writing. This method is about picking up someone else's rhythm and patterns, like copying a singer with a stronger, better-trained voice than yours. Read a selection of introductions to find your inspiration and overcome intro challenges!

heat + time = response

I designed the Reader Response Model (**RRM**) to help clients predict whether they will be read. The RRM isn't as complicated as it sounds. In fact, our simplified version considers just two factors. We've already looked at the reader's temperature. The second factor puts you in your reader's shoes by estimating how much *time* they can dedicate to your writing.

It's vital to gauge heat and time *before* you write. The RRM will give you a feel for how much you should write. And, on occasion, it will tell you not to write a single word. Let me explain, via three different readers.

Harry is boiling hot. He's desperate to read our communication. And – even better – Harry's got plenty of time to read what we write.

figure 6   RRM Says Yes

Reader Response Model					
	Very Low	Low	Medium	High	Very High
What is their temperature?					✓
How much time do they have now?				✓	

You can imagine Harry at his desk, waiting for your life-changing email to come through. He's cleared his mind of everything else. Harry's desperate for his annual pay review or exam results. It'll be cruel to not write to him.

Our second reader is a harder nut to crack. Zayn's got a very low temperature and has very little time. He's not interested in what we have to tell him and, even if he were, he wouldn't have the time to read it.

figure 7   RRM Says No

Reader Response Model					
	Very Low	Low	Medium	High	Very High
What is their temperature?	✓				
How much time do they have now?		✓			

Zayn's the guy checking his emails in the lift on the way to a vital client meeting. He's scanning through sender names and email headers, deleting those that have no relevance. A special offer for a gym in a town he left two years ago? Delete. Party invite from people he can't stand? Delete. Updated instructions for an App that Zayn has downloaded but never used? Delete, delete, delete.

The RRM suggests writing to Zayn will be a waste of time. If we do write, we have to write something extremely short that will pique his interest.

The RRM gives a split decision when we consider Niall. Niall has a fairly high temperature but, unlike Harry, he's very short on time.

figure 8 **RRM says Communicate, but there's no need for War and Peace**

Reader Response Model					
	Very Low	Low	Medium	High	Very High
What is their temperature?					✓
How much time do they have now?	✓				

We have to communicate with Niall because he's really interested in what we have to tell him. But there's simply no point in sending a hefty report. He wants the answer to his question, but not the evidence and data you've collected to back up your findings.

Niall's the trader who wants to know whether to buy or sell gold. His time pressure means he won't read pages of detailed analysis. Just send your decision – *Buy!* – saving both of you precious time.

The split decision may also tell you to drop writing in favour of speaking. Swinging by someone's desk – or even an old-fashioned phone call – may be a smarter way to get your message across. I know this is meant to be a book on business writing, but there are occasions where I have to hold up my hands and accept writing isn't the only means of communication open to you.

I'm not going to try and pull the wool over your eyes and pretend that the RRM is scientifically accurate. It can't be. It relies on your subjective assessment of two factors about someone you possibly don't know that well. It may well be that you haven't even met them. So it's always going to be a best guess.

However, experience has taught me it's a smart way to plan how much to write. It's effective because it forces you to consider the reader's needs and constraints *before* you start writing.

Want some more advice and support? You can

download the RRM at **www.smackpitch.com/
heat+time**. Use it every time you're planning to write.
Eventually, it will become something you do instinctively
each time you decide to put fingers to keyboard or pen
to paper (for the traditionalists amongst you).

the concept of cognitive cost

I once asked a bright graduate if he could reduce his eight-page report on a company's valuation to a single page. He cut the font size from 14pt to 6pt, got rid of all the headings and fiddled with the borders so he could print right up to the edges. Of course, it was absolutely impossible to read. Cognitive cost meant I filed it carefully in the bin.

Cognitive cost[3] is a cool phrase I use when teaching business writing. I tell my clients I invented the term, but in my heart of hearts I know I've copied it from someone far smarter. Genius borrows, and all that.

We are all guilty of judging books by their covers. Cognitive cost is shorthand for *everything that puts a reader off your writing*. It's what you feel when you pick

---

3 Having got to section 8 of Smack, you are allowed to pepper your everyday conversation with this phrase. Let's see if we can popularise it!

up a slide deck and see that it's full of orange text on a yellow background. Or that it's in landscape format and packed with extended sentences that leave your eyes absolutely exhausted because you are being forced to read without pause. You feel cognitive cost when you open a box of flat-pack furniture and can't tell whether you've got the instructions upside down.

To avoid putting obstacles between you and your reader, your need to know two indisputable facts about readers:

1. Readers decide whether to read or ignore in entirely predictable ways

2. We all scan much more than we used to.

9

it is terrifyingly easy to predict what gets read

People choose what to read in very similar ways. Here are some rules to help you grab – and keep – their attention

Everyone prefers to pick up a short, attractively presented report rather than something that looks shabby and poorly constructed. If the content of two competing reports is exactly the same, the one with *good design* will get more readers. It's that simple.

Readers read summaries and recommendations first. They want to know the conclusion of the report before they dig in. If your reader reads your key recommendation – and not a single word more – you can consider your communication to have been successful.

Business writing is the opposite of talking to your

friend about a movie you haven't seen yet. You need to *reveal the ending first*. You're not spoiling the plot for business readers if you tell them *Titanic* ends with the big ship sinking. They want the conclusion first, even if it's a negative one.

Readers like content pages because they want to understand the structure of the report. They automatically feel they're in safe hands because you've organised your thoughts. It's as if they want to see your scaffolding as well as the building it supports.

Readers flick through the section headings looking for areas that are relevant to them. The headlines you use at the top of pages and to break up the report play a vital part in attracting the potential reader's attention.

Anything labelled background or appendix is ignored. In fact, the Latin word *appendix* means *skip this section entirely* (this may not be true).

the unforgiving mind of the online scanner

A friend of mine, Laura, is a high-flying corporate lawyer. Blind since birth, she listens to nearly 400 emails a day through voice recognition software.

I can hear her tutting and tapping testily on the delete key before the software has even got halfway through an email header. Laura's set the playback to such a high speed that it's impossible for me to make out a single word. She makes the decision on whether to continue with an email in less than a second. The digital world is so much quicker – and harsher – than the printed world. You've got to be good, very good, to make an impact on the reader, and you've got to know how they approach online material.

Online readers can be utterly unforgiving. They're not going to read each and every word that you've lovingly laboured over. No, in just a couple of seconds their eyes will scan your article in a predictable F-shape.

They begin with the headline. They might even read the first sentence and a half, if they're feeling especially relaxed. Then their eyes dart down the left hand side of the screen looking for words or headings of interest.

At the second paragraph their eyes travel left again, though not as far as the first time. If they believe the article is of interest, they'll take a second dart down to the prong of the F.

figure 8 Readers don't even have time for the whole F word these days.

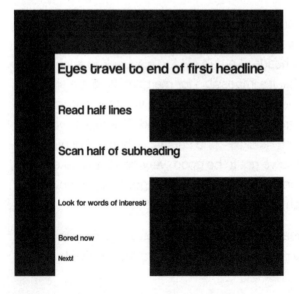

Eyes travel to end of first headline

Read half lines

Scan half of subheading

Look for words of interest

Bored now

Next!

And that, in most cases, will be that. Only one in five of your readers who reach the bottom of the F will click on the down arrow. That's right. Only twenty per cent of people go *below the fold* even with articles they like.

If we do find an online piece that we want to read in detail later, we tend to bookmark it or set a reminder. We'll then forget about it completely until we're stuck for nine hours in the business lounge of Tegucigalpa airport. But – as bitter personal experience has taught me – that's the very moment the internet connection disappears for exactly nine hours.

First impressions are so important. Every reader is busy, and all of them have far too many choices. You've got to do your very best to make sure that your writing is selected. Make your work look attractive and – to re-introduce a bit of Eighties business jargon – *user-friendly*. Increasing your awareness of how people read and scan will repay the effort many times over.

what does good design look like?

Take a look at this appeal for funding from Wikipedia. The ask yourself why is it so effective?

DEAR WIKIPEDIA READERS, **We'll get right to it: This week we ask you to help Wikipedia. To protect our independence, we'll never run ads. We survive on donations averaging out €10. Only a tiny portion of our readers give. If everyone reading this right now gave €2, our fundraiser would be done within an hour. That's right, the price of a cup of coffee is all we need. We're a small non-profit with costs of a top website: servers, staff and programs. Wikipedia is something special. It is like a library or a public park where we can all go to learn. If Wikipedia is useful to you, please take one minute to keep it online and ad-free. Thank you.**

The tone is informal but not casual. The action Wikipedia wants from readers is made clear, not just in words but also by the use of highlighting. The highlighting draws you in to the most important sentence, and if that grabs your attention you'll probably read the text that comes before and after.

You don't need a team of design gurus to jazz up your

proposals and reports. Your writing will be chosen if you just follow these five basic principles.

1. Rely on *the minimum noticeable difference*. Use just enough formatting for the reader to notice, and no more. So put it in bold, underline it, change its size or switch on italics. But don't ever do more than two of these at the same time or you'll tire out the reader and look like you've just this moment discovered the formatting bar.

2. Use *clay AND the absence of clay*. I don't want to get all Zen-master on you, but you need both to make a vase. So make sure there's some white space on every page to avoid it looking crammed. Make space your friend.

3. *Don't mix typefaces* in the same document. It's better to show you're moving from a headline to the main text with a change in size and a bit of white space than having `calibri` followed by `verdana` and then `Bauhaus 93`.

4. *Don't use wingdings*. Unless you want to be seen as an idiot. The same rule applies to stickmen.

5. *Be sparing in your use of different colours*. Writing black letters on a white background may not be especially innovative, but it's worked well for centuries.

what i think about when i think about planning

My first lesson in planning came from a fellow pupil at secondary school, Marcus Crawshaw. Marcus's aim when writing his exams was to be the first person to finish a page. I remember the rustle as Marcus flipped over the top page of his answer book, while I was still deciding what questions to pick. I also remember him looking around the Assembly Hall with a satisfied glint in his eyes.

But Marcus's decision to sacrifice quality for speed backfired. He passed some of his exams, but didn't do well enough to get to university. His failure inadvertently taught me that planning demands patience.

When given a new writing task, we're often tempted to jump straight in and get the word count rising. That's often a mistake. Hold fire until you're 100% sure of what you need to write. It's better to spend fifteen minutes deciding a chapter isn't necessary, than to spend a day writing a chapter only to delete it later.

My second influence came via a soft skills trainer. As a callow youth I worked for three years at PWC in London. I avoided many dark days of work – counting brass doorknobs in a warehouse outside Harlow was a particular low point in my stellar career – by signing up for every possible course. You name it, I was there. From *Advanced Excel* to *Beginner's Emotional Intelligence* via *Wear Your Fire Marshal Cap with Pride*.

One of the earliest courses I attended was *Improving Your Personal Efficiency*. The very first thing that the trainer, Derek Greaves, showed us was about planning. He drew two simple lines on his flip chart.

figure 9   How Derek taught me to plan

Planning   Hard Work

Planning   Hard Work

The meaning of Greavsie's little graph has stayed me with ever since (it's a shame the rest of the course was a bit boring. Mind you, it was a day away from auditing door knobs in Essex).

What was Derek's message? Planning saves time. This is especially true when you're faced with a very large document. Proper preparation – which can be a quick list of the major points or a full-blown mind map – will always reduce the time needed to finish the task.

Lack of planning is especially obvious in business writing. Readers notice it well before writers are aware of it. Planning leads to clarity, for you and for the reader. If you can't organise your thoughts, your readers will vote with their eyes and decide your thoughts aren't worth reading.

part two

writing is an
emotional
business

learn from journalists

Journalists are taught to get to the point in the first line. Follow their mantra – *who, what, when, where and why* – when communicating vital messages. Instead of drafting flowery letters of resignation, journalists fire off notes like *I'm leaving at the end of the month for a job at your major competitor because you are an idiot.* What it loses in refinement, it gains in clarity.

In the days before the internet, inky-fingered editors had to fit stories to a space in the newspaper. They didn't have time to cut individual words or reorder sentences. Instead, they'd keep paragraphs one to six exactly as they were, and then snip off the copy at the top of paragraph seven.

Readers are exactly the same. They start at the top, take what they need, and leave.

the fear index

Before we go on, I want to check where you are on the Fear Index. This index (which I've just invented) measures how afraid you are of criticism – or even failure – when it comes to your writing.

How do you feel about your starting your new assignment?

1	2	3	4	5	6	7	8	9	10
Great!	Easy	No Big Deal	Fine	OK	OKish	Nervy	Afraid	Shaking	Petrified!

Some people are blessed with confidence, so they plot themselves on the far left. But most of us are nervous about our writing. It may be that we've had bad experiences in the past, where bosses have cruelly corrected us or we've made high profile errors seen by thousands. For some, it goes all the way back to school. I was told off for poor handwriting when I was six, and again in an oak-panelled room in a fourteenth century Cambridge college, for screwing up a draft chapter of my Master's degree. I can still remember how both these events damaged my confidence.

Nerves can stop us telling our readers exactly what we think or feel about our subject. I used to write articles on finance and technology for a national newspaper. One Thursday the deputy editor ran past me.

'Hi Susan...'

But Susan's hands covered her mouth as she rushed towards the toilets. The corridor filled with the sound of retching.

'Morning sickness,' said Julian Watkins, a features writer.

'I didn't know she was pregnant.'

'She's not.' Julian pointed to the Paracetamol and the three empty coffee cups on Susan's desk. The tell-tale red cap of a Smirnoff bottle poked out from a drawer. 'It's our code for Susan's too drunk to work.'

'I see.'

'It's becoming more and more of a problem. We've six minutes to write the Market Report. I don't suppose...'

I nodded. 'Sure.'

How difficult could it be to write two hundred words in six – now five – minutes? All I needed was a killer opening line. But then a text zapped onto my phone. I tried to ignore it, tried to focus on the intro, tried not to get distracted as the text reflected in Julian's dirty spectacles. Damn, it was Susan.

Be a dear and sneak out the Vodka. Pretty please xxx.

Julian shook his head. 'Time is tight. Four minutes to go. Make that three.' I wrote six words but deleted them. The second text pinged and I felt a sheen of sweat on my forehead.

Please, Andreas, I'm dying here. And don't tell Julian!

Two minutes to go, and the vein on my forehead throbbed. I looked up at the ceiling for inspiration, but nothing came.

Susan's third text was a threat.

Get me the vodka, damn you, or you'll never work for us again. Valuable seconds – and my lucrative gig at this prestigious paper – were disappearing like water down a plughole.

One minute. My word count was still stuck at zero. How could I get so blocked in the office, when at home the ideas poured out so easily? The blank screen mocked me. Julian tapped his fingers on his desk. My phone rang. It was Susan. I ignored her and forced my twitching hands back onto the keyboard.

I began with *It's been an up and down day in the City*. Fifty seconds later, just as the clock struck four, I pressed send. The Pulitzer Prize would have to wait, but at least I'd met my deadline.

Distractions are all around us and fear makes us procrastinate. The butterflies in our stomach somehow find their way to our brains, and we can't write what we need to write. What steps can you take to get started?

Write something immediately. Just ten words may be enough to find your groove. It doesn't matter that they're the wrong words in the wrong order, because that's why the delete key was invented. The move from *I am thinking about writing* to *I am writing* is vital.

I'd like to recommend a book here. Haruki Murakami is a fantastic novelist and a fanatical marathon runner. In *What I Talk About When I Talk About Running*, Murakami discusses the similarities between writing and endurance events. Both are about getting off the sofa, taking the first steps and persevering through the pain.

Tell people that you're writing. Don't get all enigmatic and keep your ideas bottled up. Let people know your area and your approach. I always find that speaking to people about my next project immediately tightens up ideas. I can see in their face if it's a dud or a winner. And I can also hear in my own voice if an idea is underdeveloped or brilliant.

Many of us *carry around* work projects in our mind. Use your commute to mentally meander through your musings and sort out your structure. Give yourself a head start (poor pun intended) and plan your writing on the way to work.

Make sure you *accentuate the positive.* Be careful of sending yourself negative messages, such as *the deadline is too tight* or *I don't have enough content knowledge.* Our brains can only focus on one thought at time, so replace these destructive ideas with *I am making great progress* and *this is much easier than I imagined.*

The Fear Index won't solve your emotional problems, but it will increase your self-awareness. If you're giving yourself a score above six you need to know why. Without sounding like a life coach, 'check in with yourself' before you write another word. If you're tense or uninspired, then stop and relax and read the upcoming sections on writer's block and flow.

ritual, routine and regularity destroy writer's block

Have you ever suffered from Cleaner's Block? You know, your muse can't find your mop and the vacuum simply refuses to suck.

Of course you haven't.

Or what about Management Accountant's Block? The creativity you need to save your spreadsheet is lacking, so you snooze under a willow tree until divine inspiration falls into your lap.

Nope. Me neither.

What about Business Writer's Block?

Yes, I see you nodding in agreement. It's flared up again, and there's even some secondary procrastination in the diagnosis. You slump over your desk, head in hands, and moan there's nothing you can do about it. But don't despair! You can banish Business Writer's Block (BWB) forever with Ritual, Routine and Regularity (RRR).

Ritual

Do you know why writers have favourite pens and lucky cardigans? They act as cognitive cues, telling the brain it's time to write.

You probably have loads of cognitive cues that you're not aware of. Unzipping your sports bag in the gym – or jamming on your headphones before your run – are both cues for the ritual of exercise. You might have a favourite song that you play before going out on a Saturday night. 'Be young, be foolish, be happy!' is your cue to lighten up and dance around.

The strongest and most immediate cognitive cue for business writers is place. Entering this zone tells your mind to write. So find the space where you write easiest. Treat it as your writing factory. This is not the place to talk about your projects, question your creativity or bitch on Twitter about constant interruptions. No. This is where you write.

Routine

Every successful writer has a routine. But the most important aspect of all routines is clocking on. Don't waste your time waiting for the ideal moment to arrive. It probably won't.

Set yourself achievable targets. Commit to an hour of solid writing or five hundred words until you can have a tea break. Keep your motivation strong by chunking down big writing tasks into doable sections.

Regularity

For many of us, business writing is not an everyday occurrence. Drafting the Chairman's Statement for the Annual Report is like running a 10k without any training. No wonder we suffer from BWB.

Keep your writing muscles limber with regular exercise. Take on smaller writing tasks in the build-up to a megaproject. Find ten minutes every day to make an e-mail more personal or to strip away the guff from a wordy marketing pitch. Practice, practice, practice!

Finding the best combination of Ritual, Routine and Regularity is always personal. The famous Russian author, Alexander Pushkin, developed a really smart way to rid himself of writer's block. When he noticed his productivity waning, he'd write standing up at a lectern.

I freely acknowledge that most of us don't have easy access to lecterns, but the idea still works. You'll always find that ten minutes standing upright will be more beneficial than an hour and a half slumped in your chair, sleeping off lunch and doodling in your notebook. A quick stroll around the park can really lift your spirits and put your brain back into the writing mode.

Watch out for tiredness. Tired writers produce exhausted and exhausting writing. If your eyes are fluttering shut, imagine how bad it will be for your reader. Take a break, get some fresh air, and pour some coffee down your neck. If none of these steps work, call it a day and return to the writing coalface in the morning.

Maximise what works for you to steadily increase your productivity and your quality. Soon Business Writer's Block will be something that afflicts your competitors, but not you.

the monk and the rockstar

The combination of blank screen and tight deadline can be terrifying. So how can you create the best environment for your business writing? Simple. Work out if you are a monk or a rockstar.

What does the monk want? Complete silence as he lifts his fountain pen from the oak desk. Absolutely no interruptions. Shhhh!

And the rockstar? He loves the cheers of the stadium. At the after-show party his ears positively ring.

Both the monk and the rockstar have found their ideal environment. And you can do the same by considering these three factors – Time, Space and Noise.

Time

When do you find writing easy? The monk's favourite slot is early morning, just as dawn breaks through the cloister windows. The rockstar is up all night. Inspiration comes when the moon is high.

QUICK TIP – *absolutely no-one writes well in the two hours after lunch. A full stomach is the enemy of writing. To maximise your most productive slots, use the post-lunch lull for admin.*

Space

Where does your writing find its wings? The monk likes his dedicated space and hates interruptions. Writing is a solo activity. Some business writers need people around them to perform. Like the rockstar, they're nothing without an audience. A busy office gives them energy to complete their task. Their desk is where they work.

QUICK TIP – *even the biggest blabbermouth can become introverted when it comes to writing. Carving out a space you control is vital.*

Noise

Do you write more effectively with silence or with noise? Most writers aren't divas, whose fragile creative genius is destroyed by the squawk of a seagull five miles away. In my experience, complete silence can put even the most conscientious monk on edge, but writers do tend to hate interruptions. They use silence as a way to mark out their territory and may even wear headphones at work to send out a strong *disturb-me-at-your-peril* vibe.

Other people welcome short chats as a way to re-charge their energy. For them, a busy office or even a trading floor gives them a buzz. Silence sends them to sleep.

QUICK TIP – *If you want music, I recommend something you already know and love. Let's face facts. Halfway through that lengthy email isn't the best time to crack open the latest tune from Throbbing Gristle.*

Time and Space and Noise. These are the three factors that determine how efficiently you write. (It's also a great title for a self-help book.)

What conditions work well for me? I like zero interruptions, familiar music, early mornings and a clear desk. I like long stretches of focus, which I break up with tea breaks and walks outside. I use a voice recorder for sudden flashes of inspiration. Something of a stationery junkie, I keep a notepad or scratchpad close to me even when I'm working on the computer. I get irrationally irritated when I can't find my propelling pencils.

And what conditions are bad for me? Too many interruptions, late afternoons and an untidy desk. I hate sharing my writing space with others, and I can't stand the radio or TV. Writing in short bursts gets me nowhere and cheap biros make me sick. I can ignore phone calls and texts with ease, but the devil's window that is the internet destroys my productivity.

figure 11 My best conditions for writing

	Good	*Bad*
Time	Long stretches Early morning	Short bursts Afternoon
Space	Clear desk No people near me	Clutter People around me
Noise	Music No calls	Absolute silence Lots of noise

Let me confess, there's nothing overly scientific in my findings. They're based on twenty years of writing about finance and the workplace, but they're nothing more than my personal preferences.

Your next step is finding what works for you. Writing is the most personal of business skills. Invest five minutes to clarify what conditions work for you, and what conditions don't.

figure 12 Your best conditions for writing

	Good	Bad
Time		
Space		
Noise		

You've probably found out that you – like 99 per cent of the working population – are a mixture of both rockstar and monk. Unless you're already a monk or as a rockstar. In which case, you're probably not too bothered about drafting your next executive summary anyway.

finding flow

I can see two examples of flow as I write this. My six-year old daughter is utterly absorbed with copying a picture of Princess Anna into her *Frozen* drawing book. Nothing – but nothing – can break her attention. Next to her, my nephew Alex is practising on his favourite uncle's guitar (I'm his favourite uncle, if that's not sufficiently clear). He's playing Arctic Monkeys riffs far better than I ever could. He repeats each song until it sounds just like the recording. But in this case repetition isn't work to him. It's fun.

When you experience flow, time passes without you noticing. An actor gets so immersed in learning her lines that she doesn't notice dawn breaking. A Yoga practitioner is so focused on connecting her breathing to her movements that the class passes in seconds.

You will only find flow when you have a clear *objective*. It doesn't matter if it's to punch through a plank of wood with your bare hand or to stop clients dumping you for a competitor. Flow doesn't come from noodling around.

You need to know why you are writing before you begin.

Feedback also helps you find flow. When you're searching for flow, it's vital to know that you're doing well. If someone writes *thanks to your email, fixed costs are down 4% year-on-year* you know your writing is working.

Flow occurs when you *enjoy* your task. There's a world of difference between struggling with a dull book on Spanish grammar and gulping a good Rioja and talking to Spanish people in a bar. Both are challenges. But only one is fun and that – incidentally – is that one that's most likely to improve your language skills.

You'll now be asking yourself how you can get all the wonderful benefits of flow. It's all about striking the *ideal balance* between your skills and the challenge. A boring task won't produce flow and neither will an impossible one. We all need to feel that we're being stretched, but very few of us want to feel that we're being destroyed.

Let me explain how to measure your skills against the degree of challenge. There are two steps to follow.

Begin by plotting your ability level on the horizontal axis. If you think you currently have a low level of writing ability, then you will plot on the left. If you have a lot of ability and experience, put yourself on the right.

figure 13 Step 1 Your Ability

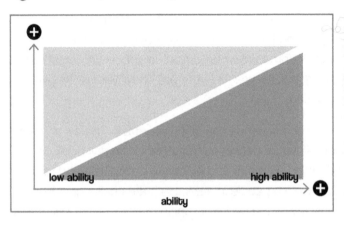

The next step is to plot the degree of difficulty on the vertical axis. This is what *you* think about the challenge, and not what other people (bosses, colleagues, flatmates) tell you.

Something super-easy, like sending the word *thanks* in an email, plots at the bottom. Something really hard – that 1,700 page appendix to the procedures manual – plots at the top of the line.

figure 14 Step 2 Your Challenge

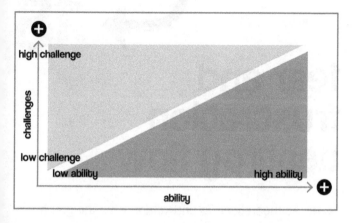

There's a downloadable version of this graph at **www.smackpitch.com**. I'd really encourage you to plot your current or next writing task so you're aware of 'where you're at'.

fear and frustration destroy flow

So far, so theoretical. To understand what the graph shows I've invented three writers – Jolene, Tom and Patsy – who plot at three very different points.

Jolene plots high in terms of challenge and low in terms of ability. She's been given something that is *too difficult* for her.

What normally happens? First of all, Jolene freezes. She can't write a single word and as the clock ticks, she begins to panic. It's impossible for Jolene to see how she can get to the end of the project. In fact, she's so tense she can't even imagine *beginning* the project.

figure 15 Fear and Loathing Destroy Flow

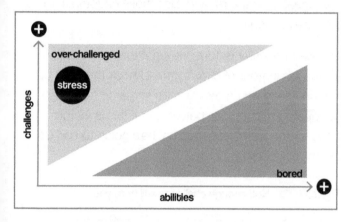

If Jolene gets too many jobs at this level of complexity she'll burn out. She may even become afraid of writing. Unless the challenge is decreased – or her writing ability goes up – Jolene will soon start looking for another job.

If you do find yourself in Jolene's position, what are the practical steps you can take to feel better?

First of all, *ask for more guidance* to define the task. Speak to the people who commissioned your work and get them to tell you more about *their* objectives. The more you know about your readers – and the more you know about what your readers need – the easier it will be to write for them.

You can also *split the task* into chunks. Instead of seeing your task as one huge report, approach it as twelve manageable chapters, and slice those chapters into discrete sections.

Our second writer is Tom. He's got too much ability for the job in front of him. Tom will knock this note out in a couple of hours because it's similar to tasks he's conquered many times before. But if this is all Tom does for the next three months, he's going to end up chronically bored.

figure 16 **Not enough challenge will bore you**

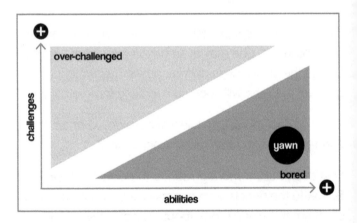

Bored writers get frustrated, then get lazy and then get irritated. And then they get irritating. You're soon going to hear Tom complain that his career isn't progressing.

How do you get away from this spirit-crushing

boredom? If writing is too easy for you, *create some pressure.* Get harder projects by convincing people you're eager to write them. Speed up mundane tasks by imposing a tighter deadline on yourself.

You can also help other writers. *Offer your skills* as an editor and – if you're good with people – think about mentoring those around you. If you're not good with people, invest the free time you've gained by learning soft skills.

enter the flow zone

Patsy is our third writer. Her level of ability matches the degree of challenge. She'll be stretched enough to feel that she's improving, but not enough to feel that the task is beyond her. This magic combination puts Patsy firmly in the channel marked *Flow*. She'll be absorbed in the task. Like my daughter and my nephew, she'll lose track of time because she's enjoying herself.

The more Patsy writes, the more her ability increases. With time, Patsy will be able to complete more challenging projects. She won't suffer the anguish that afflicts poor Jolene, nor the frustration flaring up in Tom's soul.

figure 17 The Right Stuff

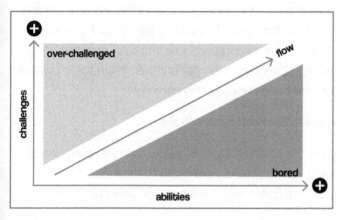

Brilliant things happen when you're in this flow zone. Your confidence zooms and your readers – and always keep your readers in mind – are much happier to read your writing. Remember what I said about feedback being important? Positive responses from your readers will boost your flow even further.

If you're not finding your flow, try *guerrilla writing*. It's far better to do thirty minutes of concentrated writing than five hours of noodling around. If you get stuck on a section move on to the next and come back when you're in flow. No first draft is perfect, so don't waste your time polishing the chandeliers while the builders are still mixing cement. At the risk of being misinterpreted, you have to bang it out quickly.

Download a new blank graph from the website. Take a minute before your next writing task to plot where you stand. Make sure that your writing task matches your writing ability. And then get another graph to plot where you are once the project is complete.

www.smackpitch.com/flow

Over the next few months, every time you commence a big writing project I want you to think about this diagram. Eventually, it will become second nature.

20

think bottom up, communicate top down

It's time to share a trade secret with you. Good business writers know that thinking is a bottom up activity, but effective communication is top down.

I'll explain in a moment. But – as a way of ramping up the tension – I want you to look at this list of twelve words. Memorise them for a minute, and then carry on reading the book.

figure 18   Twelve Words

Zurich, Love, Bing, Turnip, Joy, Sinclair, Sadness, Potatoes, Geneva, Blackberry, Asparagus, Bern

The second part of this exercise will come up in a couple of pages, so do try to be patient. In the meantime, let's talk about dating. Or – more specifically – telling your intended where you'd like to take them out. And forgive me for my patriarchal assumptions, but I'm going to explain this from the point of view of a man.

I really fancy Eliza.[4] She interviewed me for an article about behavioural finance and I found the whole process fascinating (after all, I was talking mostly about myself and what's more interesting than that, eh?). I mooched around for a couple of days before plucking up courage and pecking out a stammering email. Would she, er, be interested, er, in talking about other things. 'Sure', she replied, after a delay where each second was a torture, each minute a knife through my heart, 'Where and when?'

Men always complicate the next stage. We believe the choice of place, day and time is absolutely crucial and so we analyse many different logistical and emotional factors. I wanted to create the impression of being financially well off without being unnecessarily flash. So I looked for a place that was stylish without being formal, comfortable without being scuzzy, hip without waiters asking if I was here to pick up my great grandchildren. I had to think about price as well, and whether splitting the bill was a good or bad thing. And was it drinks,

----

4　Her real name, obviously.

dinner, dancing at the Ritz? And where should this place be?

Then I had to decide on the day. What night is good? Monday's a dead night socially, and suggests you're not giving sufficient importance to the date. Tuesday's I teach creative writing. Wednesday's good, but I know (because of my great listening skills) that it's the night Eliza goes to her German class. Thursdays are a no-no for me but what about Friday? Do I want to get drunk with her workmates? Possibly not. What about Saturday night for the date? Is that a bit risky, a bit too bold? Or does fortune favour the brave? And what's that other cliché people always use, you know the one about faint heart never winning fair hand?

I haven't even considered time. Should I be unconventional and suggest we meet in the afternoon? Or play it safe and meet at six? Or be a bit more Mediterranean and say nine? All these decisions, and I haven't even prepared a list of topics for us to talk about…

So what was in my reply? *I'll see you on Saturday at 7pm in the Hansom Bar at the Renaissance Hotel in St Pancras.* I wrote nothing about my reasoning, my doubts or the choices I considered and rejected. My reader doesn't need to know how I've come to my conclusion, but she does want to know exactly what I've concluded.

I came to my decision through a bottom up process. But my communication is top down. Just the facts, ma'am.

figure 19 Dating choices

⌄ We should communicate top down
   Saturday, 7pm. The Long Bar, The Rennaissance Hotel, St Pancras

⌃ We think bottom up
   Right impression, good day, handy location, price is right, time, days I can't go, days they can't go, too pushy, not pushy enough, too flash, not flas enough?

Enough about me. Do you remember those twelve words that you memorised? If you can recall more than eight you've doing really well (or you're cheating). If it's less than six, I don't want to criticise but you should pay more attention from now on.

Here's the surprise. The words weren't randomly selected. They fit into four different categories – abstract emotions, Swiss cities, unpopular products and vegetables.

figure 20 The Human Mind Loves to Group

Twelve Words	Category
Love	Abstract emotions
Sadness	Abstract emotions
Joy	Abstract emotions
Zurich	Swiss cities
Geneva	Swiss cities
Bern	Swiss cities
Bing	Unpopular products
Sinclair	Unpopular products
Blackberry	Unpopular products
Potatoes	Vegetables
Asparagus	Vegetables
Turnip	Vegetables

You can probably guess what I'm going to ask you to do next. I want you to remember the categories. I'll test you again, once I've told you more about my love life. Or, to be more precise, when I tell you what your author and the lovely Eliza talked about on our date.

> 'The human brain', I began, as we clinked our cocktail glasses, 'is designed to search for structure. We can turn this to our advantage when planning documents.'

> 'I see.' She took a sip. 'So you're saying we should

structure our writing to reflect how the mind thinks?'

She had both wisdom and beauty. 'Yes. Our documents should be built like pyramids. The bottom layers should explain how we reached our conclusion.'

Eliza's perfectly manicured hands rested on the arm of the leather sofa. 'Is that because we form our opinions on a bottom up basis?'

'Yes! But our opinions are best communicated via the top down approach, where we reveal our conclusion at the apex of the pyramid.'

She smiled. 'It's almost the opposite of storytelling, where the ending is not known until the final scene. With top-down communication you reveal your ending first.' Our glasses clinked again. 'So tell me, Andreas, how do you want this important conversation to end...?'

We talked long into the night. I told her how the bottom up process in business writing begins when we research. We look for evidence, search for flaws in logical arguments, collect data and crunch numbers. It's during this stage that we build up our ideas and opinions. If we can stay open-minded we'll see the pros and cons of all options. We need to sift, evaluate, accept and reject to reach our conclusion.

For our second date I asked her if she wanted to see *Titanic.* But she told me she already knew how the story ended…

The vast majority of our readers don't want to know about the bottom up stage. They want top down communication. Tell them what you've found out, not how you've found it. Yes, you do need to keep all your workings, and may even display them later in the report. But we're all in a hurry, so get your most important point across first.

There's a lot more about pyramids coming up in Part 3.

see your reader

One of the great paradoxes of writing is that the more you think about a single person, the more your writing appeals to multiple readers.

Radio DJs project towards a single listener, even if they are broadcasting to millions. By being specific, they appeal to a wide audience. In their imagination they're speaking to a woman in a factory, a man stuck in traffic or a schoolboy doing his homework. If you try to include everyone as your target audience, you'll actually think about no-one. Your writing will become dehumanised and lack colour.

As you're writing imagine you're talking to a person. Would you use Latin words or deliberately complex words or words that make them fall asleep? Of course you wouldn't. You'd choose the fastest and freshest way to get your meaning across.

A fake expert talks down to readers via his writing because he feels the need to be cleverer than them. True experts prefer to explain and inspire. They don't

assume other people are stupid because they know less
about their chosen field than they do.

Fake experts delight in using obscure words and highly
technical vocabulary. But terms that aren't recognised
break the flow of a piece. Use *franchise cronut* instead
of *brand*, and your readers will head to the net to look
up a translation. While they're searching, they'll find a
simple article on the same subject (in their mind, *simple*
equates to *better*).

Visualise a specific reader when you write. Choose
someone who's smart but doesn't know a huge amount
on the topic you're writing on. Pick someone who you
hold in high regard and who has high standards. Then
speak to them.

Visualising your reader is a godsend for both content
and tone. The copywriters employed by Apple were
great at making the costumer feel like an individual.
Their adverts stressed why humans like computers –
they help us make friends, produce art, edit videos and
send gifs of waving cats to our grandmothers. IBM, by
contrast, depersonalized their audience. Reams of detail
about memory specification and ROM/bios made it clear
you were buying a machine rather than an experience.
This was tremendously useful and interesting (and even
enjoyable) for the engineers and scientists who were

responsible for the IT budget. They wanted facts, not emotional connection.

It's easy to lose sight of the reader while we're writing. You see this happen when corporate writers forget their audience is composed of human beings. Take this example from my local swimming pool:

> **Our mission is to be the best-in-breed leisure center. To help us achieve our aims, we request that patrons kindly refrain from leaving their wet clothing and toweling on the floor of the changing room. We have provided appropriate receptacles for this purpose.**[5]

How can you improve this guff? Imagine the swimmer as a person, rather than a source of problems. Your tone and vocabulary will change even though your objective (keeping the changing rooms tidy) is exactly the same. You'll move from the general (the ugly sounding *patron)* to the specific (the much friendlier *you). Being polite (*please)* is more important than being corporate (the slightly prissy *we request). No-one cares about the leisure company's mission and aims when they're trying to find their towel in a cold dressing room. Bland words – *refrain, best-in-breed, appropriate* – make the notice

---

5   Sorry, I can't provide a photo, but no-one wants to use a camera in a gym dressing room, do they?

even more impersonal. And *receptacles,* in case you're
wondering, are *baskets.*

Time for a sweeping statement – being specific will
make you a more popular writer. Read any great novel
of personal struggle in the face of adversity and you'll
realise the more personal the details, the greater the
connection you feel with the writer.

Let me use Simon, who runs the mega-successful
T-shirt company *Shot Dead In the Head*, as an
example. Simon was planning to run a customer
services conference for his B2B staff. His original email
promised *the program/conference will contain several
opportunities to practise real-life scenarios.* Take up from
his sales force was so low as to be almost non-existent.

I told Simon, as I struggled into a large Kraftwerk T-shirt,
that his vocabulary was far too vague to create a strong
image in the minds of his sales force. He countered by
offering me an extra-large shirt (touché) and challenging
me to do a rework.

Easy. I got rid of the redundant *program/conference*
because it was already clear what event he was trying
to describe. The flabby *opportunities to practise real-life
scenarios* was tightened into *chances to practise your
sales pitch.* I changed the vague *several* to the more
concrete *five.* I switched the subject from *program/*

conference to *you,* which made the humans the most important part of the sentence.

You will get five chances to practice your sales pitch.

Examples are a fine way to move from the general to the specific. Even if – as in this case – you need to emphasise certain details to make your point more memorable. And just so you know, the extra-large shirt was actually a little baggy around the midriff.

Too many abstract words – *effectiveness, compliance,* anything ending in *-centric* – dull your writing. There's nothing for the reader to grasp, kick around or bite into. Details move people to action, whilst generalities put them in a coma.

How can you be more concrete? Use words that evoke senses. Imagine you are on holiday in Italy and want to escape from the searing Tuscany sun. You push open the door to the delicatessen on the corner and breathe in that magical mix of ground coffee beans and bitter-sweet Amaretto biscuits. Pick up a chunk of Parmigiana and hold it up to your nose. Notice your body changing as your mouth begins to water…and now feel the crushing agony when you get an email beginning *the recent contraction in catering facilities will result in an alleviation of solution delivery issues.*

your most important point always comes first

Always, always, always. When you send an email, make sure your header tells the readers why they should read it. If you write a twelve-page note on what accounting package the firm should buy, highlight your final recommendation on the first page. And if you've spent six months analysing whether your company should buy out a competitor, your reader must be able to immediately find the words *yes* or *no*.

You never know who will end up reading your work. Imagine the CEO of Mega Corp striding past your desk on the way to a meeting of immense global significance. He sneezes and, while looking for a tissue to blow his nose, glances down at the bombsite that is your desk. He sees the cover of your report. In this single second

– the only time he's ever noticed your miserable, pitiful existence – what do you think he wants to read?

A – this report into gold was produced using our standard methodology

B – fill your boots with gold!

He wants B (your findings) not A (your workings). If he likes your findings, he may well read how you arrived at your opinion. But if you lead off with your method, he'll never get to your answer.

If the most important person in the company knows what you're thinking, then your report has succeeded.

Do you remember Eliza, my hot date, and her wise words about top down communication and bottom up thinking? The pyramid is a winner because it starts with your most important point (the top) and also allows you to present your backup information (the bottom) in a clear way.

Readers feel comfortable when a report is clearly structured. They love moving from your key recommendation into sections, chapters and modules.

In my experience, relatively few people reach the end of your report. But those who get there demand huge amounts of detail. Contrast that against the main recommendation, which is read by many people but has very little detail.

figure 21 Top and Bottom Compared

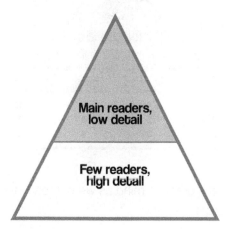

Let's finish with those twelve words. I'm now going to give you a pyramid to fill in. Your brain will remember more words – even though time and pages have passed – because of the structure.

figure 22 The Mind loves Structure

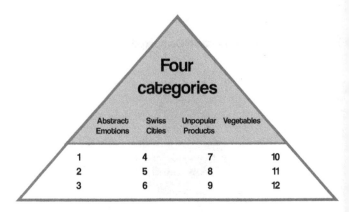

Keep this little graph in mind as we get ready to talk about stucture.

part three

structure

pyramids have never gone out of fashion

The pyramid structure is an absolute must for your longer pieces of writing. You start at the top, then you support your most important point with layers of evidence, opinion, data, research and facts.

Every level below the apex must reinforce your recommendation. In our Mega Corp example, the bold assertion *fill your boots with gold* needs to be backed up.

Typically, the next level of the pyramid contains two, three or four bricks. Each one must explain how you reached your recommendation.

figure 23 Gold

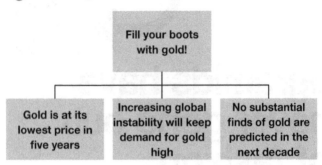

Do you remember what it felt like when you realised Father Christmas didn't exist? You were upset of course, and you might have even shed a tear or two. But you also experienced relief because you didn't have to pretend any more.

You'll probably feel the same mixture of emotions now when I tell you that no-one is going to read your entire report. It simply won't happen. But you can turn this apparent problem into a huge advantage.

Stick with me. I will explain how the pyramid structure actually creates more readers for your report, not less. To do this, we need to talk about the two greatest movies ever made, and their not very good sequel. Roll up, ladies and gentlemen, for the *Godfather Trilogy*.

I've done my research by watching these films many times. I can voice my overall conclusion at the top of the pyramid with confidence – *Godfather 1 and 2 are far better than Godfather 3*. But I need to back this up for people who don't trust me as a film critic. So level two of my pyramid gives a little depth to my opinions – *Why Godfather 1 is Great, Why Godfather 2 is the Best Movie Ever Made* and *Why Godfather 3 is Rubbish*.

figure 24   **The Godfather Movies**

You'll now see the beauty of the pyramid. If my film mate, Vanessa, is interested in 1, 2 and 3 she can read the next layers, where I attempt to justify each of these opinions.

However, if she already knows 1 was great, there's no need for Vanessa to continue with this section. She can jettison this chapter and, with the time she's saved, she can read more about 2 and 3.

figure 25   The Godfather Movies

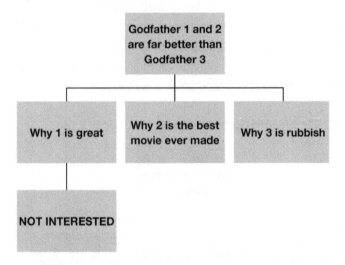

The pyramid structure helps Vanessa find the logic behind my decision. She might not agree with me, but she will see that I've properly considered the subject and not just banged down an ill-informed rant.

Let's add another layer, where I attempt to justify my opinions. I love 2 for its themes and its narrative. I hate 3 because of its acting (for the sake of simplicity, I'm not going to mention 1 again).

figure 26　The Godfather Movies

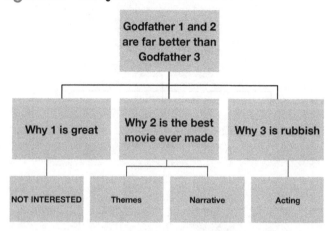

Vanessa is now satisfied by my opinion on 2. She won't spend her time reading either of the sections that support my critique. But she does need more evidence before I can convince her about 3. I need to add another layer. As evidence of quite excruciating acting I'll put forward the scene where Sofia Coppola makes gnocchi with her love interest, played by Andy Garcia, and any scene where Andy Garcia bites his knuckle in frustration.

The way I've structured the report allows Vanessa to find exactly what she needs. It's as if I've tailored the report to her exact needs. And there's a kicker. Other readers can find exactly what they want as well. Everyone feels like it's tailored for them.

figure 27   The Godfather Movies

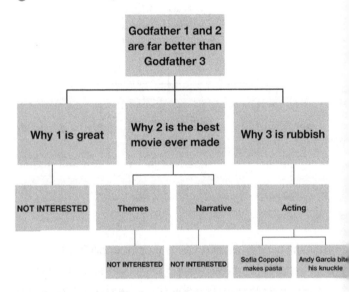

Those of you with good memories will now also be thinking of abstract emotions, Swiss cities, unpopular products and vegetables. One of the huge advantages of using the pyramid is that it mimics the brain's urge to form groups. The pyramid structure is always a winner with readers because it instantly organises ideas.

The pyramid structure ensures your report appeals to many readers with many different needs. But to make it work, you need to add some signposts.

signposts guide your readers

Did you see what I did there? The line above this one sums up the entire paragraph below. Whether you call them headings or sub-headers, they direct your reader through your report.

Have you ever watched a reader when they're lost? It's awful. They turn back a page, screw their eyes up, scratch their head and wonder why they can't follow the argument. Because you haven't structured your report well, they start to question whether you truly understand the content. You might hear some tutting. *What is this idiot on about?* they'll say, as your report falls to the floor and you lose another reader.

Signposting solves their anger and frustration by making your pyramid explicit. I'll teach this by telling you more about the structure I've chosen for the very book you have in your hands now.

The main aim of *Smack Your Pitch Up!* is to make your

business writing better. The book splits into six sections, which I refer to as *parts.* In each part there are either ten or twelve chapters, which I'm calling modules because I don't want to sound old-fashioned. You'll have noticed I divided most modules (especially the longer ones) with subheadings.

Your Title	*Smack Your Pitch Up!*
Main aim, conclusion or recommendation	Makes your business writing better
Section Headings	The Reader Comes First Writing is an Emotional Business Structure Crafting Your Style Words, words, words Happy Endings
Chapter Titles	The 10-12 modules in each section
Subheadings	The lines, words and phrases you see in italics at the beginning of paragraphs

Most subheadings I read are fairly bland and uninformative. Making these *labels* work hard for you needs time and skill. Let's focus on turning subheadings into signposts. Here are three trumpet-blowing examples for you to consider:

figure 28 Three Types of Sub-Header

Label   Smack Your Pitch Up is a book on
                business writing

Question   What makes Smack Your Pitch Up
                better than other books on business
                writing?

Pull Quote Smack Your Pitch Up is concise, funny,
                useful and written with modesty

One tip is to turn subheadings into *questions*. It's OK to
write Copper Prices at the top of a paragraph, but it's
more engaging to turn the subheading into the question,
Have Copper Prices Peaked? The next paragraph
should flow easily because you're now obliged to
answer the question immediately.

'Buy this book'

One technique that's underrated it to change your
subheading into *pull quotes*. Pull quotes are brief
summaries, never more than half a line long, at the
top of sections and major paragraphs. When you
flick through the business biographies and popular
psychology books in WHSmith, you'll see a pull quote
every three or four pages. They're in a bigger font than
the rest of the text and should turn a warm reader –

someone who's already read the cover and the blurb on the back – into a hot reader who wants to buy this book.

Make your headings work for skimmers

Some people want to read your report solely through its headings. Starting at your front cover with your main recommendation, they should be able to understand your thoughts by reading headlines, subheadings, questions and pull quotes. Not every word has to be read for your report to be a success. A flick through may well be enough to convince.

are you about to write the perfect headline?

People scan headlines in the same brutal way they flick through pictures on Tinder. The decision to read is made in less than a second. Our eyes focus on the first three words and the last three words of any headline, so you need your most important words in these two locations. Look at this:

Perfect headlines exist for online posts if you follow these essential writing tips

It's wordy and commits the mortal sin of running over into a second line. The headline will have much more impact once it's cut down to six words. Remember, readers read the first three and last three words. The less words in a headline – and the shorter they are – the greater the chance that readers will dive in (this will also help with SEO, where the title tag has to contain less than 55 characters to avoid being abbreviated in search results).

My stripped-back version now reads:

Essential writing tips for perfect headlines

A quick scan through clickbait articles reveals three common techniques that also work:

1. Question – *do you know the rules for perfect headlines?*

2. Numbers – *six tips for perfect headlines*

3. Personal appeal – *for people just about to write the perfect headline*

Use these to add variety to your subheadings, but be careful of over-doing them.

learning from the charity muggers

You see them in every High Street and shopping mall of the world. With their big fake smiles, bright T-shirts and friendly clipboards, the charity collectors are hugely talented at parting us from our hard-earned money.

I'd just taken a fistful of notes from an ATM in Bruges when I came face to face with Juliette. She was raising funds for cancer nurses but each nurse cost €24 per hour. If I texted just €2, I'd cover the cost of a nurse for five minutes.

'What can you get for just two euros these days,' Juliette said, 'that will make you feel so good about yourself?' My pocket was bulging with cash after the visit to the cashpoint. 'Two euros is a tiny amount when you compare it to what a life-saving nurse does.'

Each collector – or 'chugger' as they are more commonly known – has a target of between ten and twenty-five texts per day. At two euros a time that's hardly enough to cover a single nurse for two hours. But once I'd sent a text I was a supporter of the charity. I was committed. And that commitment is how the charity company makes their corn. Three days later Juliette rang and asked me to sign up for a monthly direct debit.

'You've already shown you believe in the cause,' Juliette said.

I didn't sign because I knew the numbers. On average, people keep paying a direct debit to a charity for four years. By which time they'll have handed over €480. Not a bad return on investment when you consider that the chugger earns no more than eight euros an hour. And the collection company takes at least a year of your money as commission.

To achieve their targets, charity collectors follow a well-defined four-stage plan when they're pitching – the **SCQA**. Let's take a look at how this works with a second example. Again, I'm sticking with the world of medicine.

Situation – more people are waiting for a kidney transplant than ever before

Complication – many donor families are unable to give the gift of life after their loved one has died because they can't find the donor card

Question – what can be done to increase the supply of kidneys in an ethical way?

Answer – switch to an opt-out system, where donation is presumed unless stated otherwise. This will increase the supply of kidneys – as well as hearts, lungs, livers and corneas – for people currently suffering on the waiting list.

This four-stage model works because it changes what you think (*I didn't know about the number of people waiting*), before making you change the way you act (*I can put my name to a direct debit form*). Every word in this rapid pitch works hard to make you donate.

make your introduction write itself

Many writers hate introductions. The blank screen stares threateningly at us, daring us to write and delete, write and delete. We feel butterflies in our stomach and search around desperately for something – anything – to do instead. But those days of fear and procrastination are over if you follow the SCQA approach.

The charity collecting companies didn't become rich without being smart. They base their scripts on the SCQA introduction, which is a classic way to begin reports.

You start with a *situation*. Your reader should recognise and – hopefully -agree with this statement. Then you muddy the waters with a *complication*. This is something that will, at a minimum, upset the status quo. At worst, the complication warns of an impending disaster. Next you hit your reader with a *question*. By now the reader's interest should be so sufficiently piqued that they're salivating for the *answer.* This answer is your main point, key finding, or overriding message.

Let's apply the SCQA to business. You have been charged with turning round a holding company whose brands are exhausted. The rest of the board is pushed for time. How can you succinctly present your findings?

figure 29 The SCQA Introduction Works Every Time

Situation
• Our portfolio of products no longer provide organic growth
Complication
• Sales will decline more because our products are associated with an older demographic
Question
• How can we achieve growth without disrupting our existing portfolio?
Answer
• Acquire other brands which can be incorporated with the minimum of disruption

The SCQA forces you to clarify your argument. Best of all, it makes your most important message completely clear. The A in the SCQA should be on the front cover of all your reports from now.

three steps to summary heaven

Remember Useful, Interesting and Enjoyable from Part One? We need to provide reasons for the reader to choose our work, and we need these reasons to be clear straightaway. I use a three-stage approach to produce summaries that grab attention.

Step one is the *elevator pitch*. Most of you will have come across this in your courses on client relationships or presentation skills, and you may well wonder what relevance it has to business writing. Simple. You are now selling your writing to everyone who passes your desk.

Instead of a minute in the lift, you have a minute with three small boxes. What I'd like you to do is to consider your next substantial piece of writing. Fill each of these three boxes with a recommendation, conclusion or key point. To force you to keep it brief, you're not allowed to let your writing cross a border.

Your minute starts now.

figure 30 Elevator Pitch

Point 1	
Point 2	
Point 3	

Step two puts you under more pressure. I want you to summarise your report as a *tweet*. Tweeting to me remains a slightly mysterious form of communication, but one advantage I see is that it forces people to nutshell (I apologise profusely for my use of *nutshell* as a verb, but stick with me. I like the word because it suggests a lot of meaning in a very small space).

A tweet forces you to explain your message in only 140 spaces. Those 140 spaces have to contain letters, punctuation and spaces. I'm giving you even less space because you need to include my name (I'm @looEzoo) and the hashtag #smackpitch!

Because of these tough constrictions, I want you to tweet your single most important idea. It'll be the only tweet I get this year, so please do it.

figure 31 Tweet

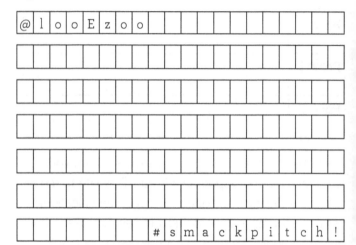

| @ | l | o | o | E | z | o | o | | | | | | | | | | | | |

| | | | | | | | | | | | | | | | | | | | |

| | | | | | | | | | | | | | | | | | | | |

| | | | | | | | | | | | | | | | | | | | |

| | | | | | | | | | | | | | | | | | | | |

| | | | | | | | | | | | | | | | | | | | |

| | | | | | | | # | s | m | a | c | k | p | i | t | c | h | ! | |

Step three is the toughest. I want you to imagine you write those banners you see outside stations. You have seconds to convince a cold reader to choose your free newspaper rather than a competitor's.

Because these adverts need to be visible from a distance, they use big letters. So your banner has a maximum of four lines, and each line has seven spaces. To get your message across you need short words.

Headline writers are expert in compressing a lot of meaning into a small number of letters. Here are some examples of tabloidese to get you in the mood:

Normal Use	Headline
Prohibition	Ban
Prime Minister	PM
Terminate	End
Europe	EU
North America	US
David Beckham	Becks
Jennifer Lopez	J-Lo
Andreas Loizou	A-Lo

Now go back to your tweet and turn it into a banner advert.

figure 32 Read all about it

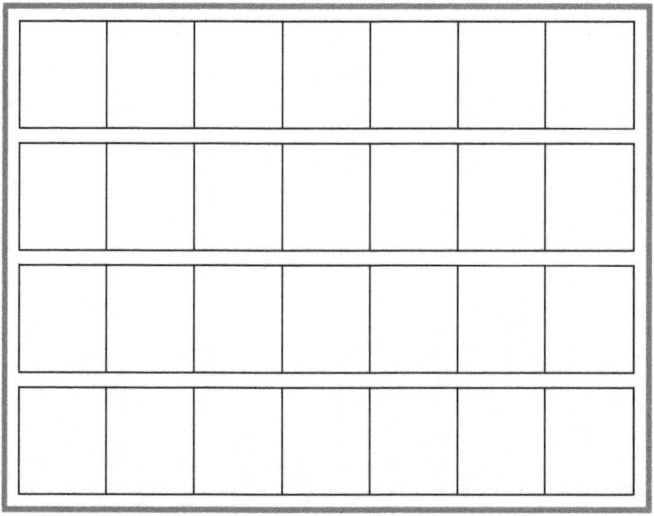

Are you surprised at how easy it is to produce summaries? Working with constraints forces you to be concise. Or, as you might now prefer:

Word Cuts Force Clarity.

the rules of readability

Nobody's ever asked you to make a sentence more complicated, have they?

A lot of research has gone into measuring the ideal sentence length for business writing. There are many lessons to be learned from linguistic experts, but their major findings can be summarised in two bullets:

1. Short sentences are best

2. It's absolutely essential to vary the length of your sentences

The ideal sentence is only *eight words* long.

A sentence should be long enough to express a single idea, but no more. If you find yourself trying to cram too many ideas into a sentence, you probably need more sentences. Too many really long sentences make the reader sleepy and confused. But too many short sentences irritate readers, and they may also suspect that you're a little bit of an idiot. Got that? Great. Now read on.

If you write more than *fifteen words* you'll lose 10% of your readers.

At *twenty words*, a quarter of your readers will have to re-read the sentence again or they won't understand it.

Anything longer than *twenty-five* words (which is two-to-three lines in this book) will make readers struggle and, unless they're really keen on moving through a morass of clauses, they'll find something easier and more rewarding to read, and all your hard work will be wasted, leaving you frustrated, tearful and even reluctant to write another word.

It's a myth that a difficult subjects leads to difficult writing. The denseness of your writing is defined by two factors that are completely under your control:

1. The length of your sentences

2. Your choice of words

We'll look at your choice of words in Part Five, so let's think more about producing clear sentences. One tip I give to business writers is to aim for a level of complexity suitable for a clever student aged between sixteen and nineteen. Not a genius, but someone who's doing well during the last years of secondary education. Every reader is different, but you'll keep most of them on your side if you aim for an average of fifteen words per sentence and paragraphs shorter than ten lines.

When you read a novel, you tend to perk up when you see a section of snappy dialogue after four pages describing the weather in torturous detail. Why? The lines are shorter, there's more conflict and more action. Your eye zooms through the white space. Exactly the same happens with your business writing. Use short paragraphs to give momentum. Readers like the sensation of making progress through a document.

I want to stress your business writing should be easier to read than academic writing. Academic writing is a way for experts to communicate very complex ideas to other experts in their field. It's sort of a code. A single word or phrase – *nocebo effect* springs to mind – can contain a vast amount of meaning for an academic. Your writing must be different because it's likely to be read by people who lack such specialist knowledge. The lethal combination of long sentences and very technical terms is something to be avoided.

Many recent graduates find the transition to business writing difficult. They'll use vocabulary and constructions that brought them praise from their supervisors and tutors. This is completely understandable, but when it comes to business writing shorter is always going to be better.

Measuring your readability

There are two well-known statistical methods for analysing the complexity of your writing. The Gunning FOG index and a test called the Flesch Reading Ease (FRE) both produce a score based on the length of sentences and the number of syllables in words. You don't need to know the maths behind these calculations. Simply copy your text into gunning-fog-index.com or readability-score.com to get the assessment.

Banish any thoughts about 'dumbing down'. Readability is all about making complex subjects easier for your readers to understand.

learn from the storytellers

Great storytellers guide you to the gold. Their choice of connecting words stops the reader from getting lost. What would fairy tales be without the phrases *once upon a time* and *they all lived happily ever after*?

Great business writers know how to connect paragraphs. When paragraph two supports and agrees with paragraph one, begin with linking words like *additionally, also, furthermore* and *similarly.* But if paragraph two disagrees with paragraph one, you need a dividing word like *however, yet, despite* and – without wishing to state the obvious – *but.*

You can guide your reader through your work with words that suggest a journey. Imagine that you are giving your reader directions as they 'walk through' your report. Use *next, then* and *before* as if you were telling them how to find the train station. When you're describing something extremely technical, use direction words. Simple words – *first, second, here, there* – take your reader by the hand. Words that hint at the passage of time – *afterwards, at the same time, immediately, after a long delay* – are also beneficial.

Readers appreciate it when you signpost the end of your work. The phrase *in conclusion* always reminds me of a school science report, but *finally, to sum up* and *to close* are all good alternatives.

Your reader decides where he/she stops reading, but you decide where you stop writing. In an ideal world, of course, these would be at exactly the same place. Ask yourself if the reader loses anything if you cross out the last paragraph. If the answer is no, then delete it.

paragraphs for fun and profit

Paragraphs group together connected sentences. There's a hidden structure to strong paragraphs.

Begin with the topic sentence

The first sentence should either be an introduction (*hey, this is a new thing*) or somehow linked with the paragraph that came before it (*as I was just saying* or *but the opposite may also be true*).

The topic sentence plants the seed for the rest of your paragraph. It's used to summarise the most important aspect of the paragraph or to introduce your unique point of view.

Your readers need their interest piqued from the first line. Using questions gets them curious. Specific details, new information and a provocative opinion can all build a strong lead. It's definitely not the place for background and methodology.

Get to the point

There's a tendency to begin emails with guff like *I am writing this email because…* This is especially frequent in emails to large groups on sensitive subjects. Some writers reckon it makes them sound more serious and/or caring, but it's nothing more than throat-clearing.

Look at this example, copied from a (soon to be ex-) client's 'think piece' on LinkedIn:

Firstly I concede that I am presenting a personal view. I believe in both financial prudence and economic conservatism, but even so it is my wish to avoid partiality when discussing how an individual's moral code impacts on their saving and spending patterns. It's my contention that the most important lesson is that financial behaviour is learned from our parents.

I've put the actual content in italics in case you can't find it after the fifty-three (count 'em) words of procrastination. Even a monk reading William Caxton's first print run would have considered this a slow start. In the age of instant transmission, such a flabby introduction is unforgivable.

Play around with sentence order

Don't get fixated on the ideal length of a paragraph,

because it probably doesn't exist. I've recommended ten lines as an upper limit, but ignore this (rather arbitrary) suggestion if it doesn't work for your piece of writing. Far better to concentrate on clarity.

CTRL/C and CTRL/V are you friends here, allowing you to try out different orders. If a paragraph is still a mess after you've reviewed it a few times, the problem may be your subject knowledge rather than your writing skills. In the wise words of the Tom Tom Club, *a person who can't say what they mean, don't mean what they say*. Mind you, they also advised us *to eat your words, but don't go hungry* so I don't think we can trust all of their sage advice.

Are you left with sentences that don't fit in? It may well be that they're not needed because they don't add anything to the reader. Early drafts often contain text that's more for the writer than the final reader. Ideas we've rejected and examples that don't back up our findings can all be cut.

stuck in the middle?

The midpoint in any book is normally a stressful time for writers. We worry if it's up to scratch. Abandon or soldier on, scrap or tweak, stick or bust?

This module was one of the last additions to the book. By the time I wrote it I'd already revised the entire manuscript three times. I'd read it aloud and responded to feedback from three people. So I was in full-on review mode when I stopped for a second and reflected; how do I evaluate my own drafts?

It's tricky. After a fair amount of thinking I came up with the five factors that carry most weight for me.

1. **Powerful Start** – bang! My main recommendation is immediately stated or I've piqued interest

2. **Strong structure** – readers can find exactly what they need

3. **Narrative** – readers are taken on a journey

4. **Signposts** – headings, pull quotes and questions
   guide the reader

5. **Skills** – design, sentence length and word choice
   make it enjoyable

Nothing has been chiselled in granite, and it's easy to
go back and change individual sentences. But halfway
through any project I do like to sit back and reflect on
my original objectives.

part four

crafting your style

the difference between style and content

The smarter ones among you will have noticed that I haven't asked you to write too much yet. But now you're at the stage where you have to focus on your actual writing.

Style – as someone fabulous like Bryan Ferry probably once said – reflects your personality and your attitude. Business writing is infamous for its terrible style. We've all picked up reports because of their content, only to jettison them within seconds because of their style. A good writer can reverse this. A writer's style can be so great that it turns uninspiring content into something enjoyable.

Writing style isn't about showing off or talking down. Aim for a conversational tone, but don't be casual. Always keep in mind that writing offers huge advantages over presenting. You have time to contemplate your thoughts and reword your opening. You can search for exactly the right word, try out different sentence orders and wait for witty adlibs to bubble up in your imagination.

I'm going to show you the nuts and bolts of business writing. And hopefully you'll pick it up more easily than I have simple chords, lead licks and arpeggios in my guitar lessons over the years. We'll go down to the level of choosing one word over another. Part four is all about the details.

transition words

There are two failings that make readers complain that your writing is disjointed and they can't follow your train of thought. Either your ideas are disorganised (in which case you need to plan more) or your explanation of these ideas is weak (in which case you need to add more transition words).

Transition words are part of a writer's style. They tell readers how ideas are connected and which points are most important. They prepare us for a sudden change in direction, the appearance of a new idea or a conclusion.

Transition words move your reader from one place to another. They're the unobtrusive worker bees of your writing, weaving together your paragraphs in a smooth and reliable way. You underestimate them at your peril. Good transition words don't clamour for the reader's attention, but their absence is always noticed.

Use *time transitions* to clarify the chronology of events. These words and phrases make it easy for your reader to follow a story.

figure 33 Time transitions

In the past

Back in the day

Before Emily started as CEO

Just before the Christmas sales ended

After speaking to his team

You use *sequence transitions* to guide readers through a process. If a process is especially complicated, reduce your sentence length and add more sequence transitions.

figure 34 Sequence transitions

Next

Lastly

Then

When it's ready

At this stage

In conclusion

Cause and effect transitions tell your reader why things happened. Don't underestimate the power of these simple words and phrases, especially when explaining the impact of a decision.

figure 35   Cause and effect transitions

Because

Since

As a consequence

Due to

Resulting in

Leading to

Causing a

Point of view transitions introduce counter-opinions. They show the reader you've considered, say, the impact of budget cuts on every stakeholder, or how a board reshuffle will have repercussions on different departments. Without POV transitions you will appear scatter-brained and unfocussed. With them, you'll come across as a writer whose work is open-minded and displays a logical structure.

figure 36 Point of View transitions

Looking at the problem from…

If I was in their shoes…

From a different perspective…

Others believe…

Another way to think about this…

To play devil's advocate…

On the bright side…

Some transition words are used for introducing *additional information*

figure 37 Additional information transitions

Also

Similarly

Moreover

Furthermore

This is a good place to add

As well as

Be careful of stupidly-long transitions. These'll make
you sound like an absent-minded professor who is filling
dead air with redundant words.

Avoid	Use
Accordingly	So
At a later date	Later
At this moment in time	Now
Consequently	So
For the purpose of	To, for
Frequently	Often
In addition to	Also
In order to	To
In relation to	About
On a regular basis	Often
Prior to	Before

Transition words turn your ideas into sentences. These
sentences, in turn, will be woven into well-structured
paragraphs.

four ways to create strong sentences

Certain sentence patterns send out a strong message that your structure – and, therefore, your thinking – is logical. At the risk of overdoing the metaphor, your pyramid needs strong foundations if it's to support your recommendation.

I'll show you how to create that strong base while we visit Yoga Revolution, a fantastic studio in the middle of Madrid. The staff construct sentences in four different ways to reduce any appearance of randomness (not that they're the random type, obviously).

Problem and solution

The writer describes a challenge, and then immediately resolves the issue.

The studio's yoga teacher, Cecilia, writes to the owner,

Dharma, using the problem/solution formula. She's worried. *We don't have enough members, so we should advertise for more.*

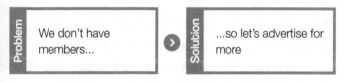

This construction makes Dharma believe he's in safe hands. Readers are reassured to hear questions raised and then immediately answered.

Cause and effect

Begin a sentence with *if* or *when*, and then show the consequences. Dharma has a different idea for Cecilia to consider. *If we run a two-for-one special offer for new joiners, we'll get an average of twelve new joiners per month.*

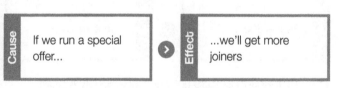

The result flows either from the current situation or the action you want to take. This construction is good for motivating people to change course or accept new ideas.

Comparison across time

This is a classic storytelling technique which has two variations

Then and now – Alison, who helps runs the business, compares her current income stream against her previous studio. She's happy. *Last year I was living off two classes a day, and now I've got five classes.*

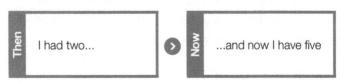

Now and the future – the owner, Dharma, contrasts the current situation with his plans for the future. He's worried. *I'm currently paying three hundred a week in rent, but next year it'll be five hundred.*

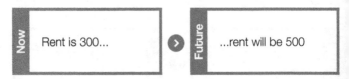

The comparison across time is marvellously logical. Use it for explaining plans, timescales and the impact of changes. Don't be afraid to use simple words – *now, then, next, before* – to increase clarity.

Compare and contrast

This is the best way to present mathematical data.

Numbers and ratios have most meaning when they are compared to trends, competitors, past results and future expectations. Your reader wants to understand how data changes, so start with the base number and then compare against the current.

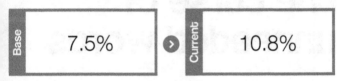

Dharma's accountants are pleased with how the studio is growing. They use the compare and contrast formula to show how performance has improved. *Last year's target was 7.5%, but now your net profit margin is 10.8%.*

How do you know you've got to the bottom of the pyramid? It's when all the data, evidence and assumptions you need to back up your recommendation at the top of the pyramid have been used.

the curse of unneeded words

Certain verbs bloat your writing without adding more meaning. There's no difference between *I am going to tell you* and the shorter *I will tell you.* But that *going to* adds an unnecessary stutter to your writing. Superfluous auxiliaries – *going to, hope to, aim to* – sow the seeds of doubt in your reader's mind. They suggest that you're not entirely convinced by your own writing.

When people write *this report aims to show* instead of *this report shows* it reminds me of a speaker nervously clearing their throat before a presentation. To be an authoritative writer, get rid of safety blankets like *I hope to* and *we aim.* We use these extra verbs and lengthier constructions because we think they sound more polite, but the real politeness in business writing is saving your reader time by getting to the point.

Business writers often expand simple words into pompous phrases by adding an unneeded *make* or *made.* Instead of writing *Khalid reported to the board*, you often read *he made a report to the board.*

A simple rule strips away this verbiage. If you wouldn't dream of saying it, don't write it. So it's *observe* not *make the observation,* and *refer to* not *make a reference to.* Just remember that *Tim made an adjustment to the invoice means exactly the same as Tim adjusted the invoice.*

Many phrases that are common in business writing can be replaced by a single word. It's all too easy when we're writing a first draft to slip these lengthy phrases into our work. The editing phase is when you should discard them, replacing them with a single word or a pithier phrase.

Shorter will always be better.

clause confusion

I was going to call this section *Clausetrophobia,* but I'm not stooping to low level puns to keep you reading.

A clause is a unit of words that includes at least one verb and a subject. A sentence can be made up of a single clause (*I want it now*) or can have multiple clauses (*I want to show you how he was able to convince the suppliers to offer us such a big discount which we can pass on to our customers*).

Too many clauses in the same sentence always create confusion. Look at this stinker from McDonald's President and CEO, Steve Easterbrook, as he announces *the initial steps to reset and turn around* the chain:

> As we look to shape McDonald's future as a modern, progressive burger company, our priorities are threefold – driving operational growth, returning excitement to our brand and unlocking financial value. The immediate priority for our business is restoring growth under a

new organizational structure and ownership
mix designed to provide greater focus on the
customer, improve our operating fundamentals
and drive a recommitment to running great
restaurants. As we turn around our business,
we will look to create more excitement around
the brand and ensure that we build on our rich
heritage of positively impacting the communities
we serve.

Forget the hideous bizspeak words if you can, and look
at the pile up of clauses. Sentence confusion doesn't
inspire any confidence in the CEO. Nobody involved
in this paragraph – the company, the PR agency, the
reviewers, the editors and, most of all, the readers – has
any idea what he's talking about. And that makes for a
very expensive waste of time.

Throughout this book I recommend you write shorter
sentences. Remember what we agreed about ideal
sentence lengths? Sentences with multiple clauses
need pruning. Cut them down or split them up to boost
readability.

passives are to be avoided

I'm writing this at Gatwick Airport. Some bright spark has circulated a questionnaire, asking us what we think about our customer experience whilst we're corralled through customs. *Your feedback would be welcomed* it says. I wanted to write that it was far better to say *we welcome your feedback*, but the sheet was already rammed full of swear words and there was no place to express my opinion.

Passives appear far too frequently in business writing. The passive voice takes an active sentence structure and turns it round. *I called the boss* is an active sentence and its passive version is *the boss was called by me*. To get all technical for a moment, the object of the active sentence (*the boss*) becomes the subject in the passive.

Passive exist to change a sentence's focus. Instead of *the clients enjoyed the presentation,* we can stress that *the presentation was enjoyed by the clients.* If the object (*presentation*) is the most important part of the sentence, put it in the position of emphasis.

Passives weaken your writing in two ways. Firstly, they automatically increase your word count. The passive voice is always longer than its active equivalent. If you want your writing to be punchy, go active rather than passive.

The second danger is that passives reduce your authority as a writer. The passive voice sends a signal that you don't want to accept responsibility. Politicians and business people often use a passive voice when they're trying to disclaim responsibility for a disaster they've created. A true apology begins with *we created a disaster.* A false one employs the passive *a disaster was created*.

why is grammar so important?

I'm one of the few native speakers to have studied English grammar. During the summer holidays I used to teach English to children from the Continent who had been sent to Margate, of all places, to brush up their skills. I studied modern English linguistics and phonetics as part of my undergraduate degree. But I'm a bit nervous about this section, and I'll tell you why.

No-one likes a grammar geek. No-one has ever found love, fame, or fortune by pointing out the errors of others. It's hard to make friends and influence people if everyone thinks you're an elitist and a pedant. Hold yourself out as a grammar expert, and people will take immense pleasure in tearing your work to shreds in the quest for errors.

A client of mine runs a company that offers services to various celebs when they come to London. He handles a certain type of business person – it could be the scion of a rich Korean family who's opening a restaurant in Knightsbridge, or a golfer who now wants work as a TV pundit. They're all happy to spend a fortune on personal brand consultants and stylists but their press releases show they consider grammar to be beneath them. Even if we're not grammar experts, we connect poor grammar with laziness. We can't help judging a person with poor punctuation as careless or – let's be frank – a bit stupid.

Grammar and punctuation stop your sentences from falling apart. Too many business writers treat them as optional extras. They're the writers who haven't realised how good grammar adds clarity to their writing (as you already know, greater clarity leads to more readers). We don't have time for a full grammar and punctuation guide here. But I want you to have tips that will immediately improve your writing. You've got to get these right if you want to keep readers on your side.

grammar's greatest hits

This is unlikely to be your favourite part of the book, so I'll focus on the two most common errors I come across. I've included one of the world's worst jokes in history to keep your attention on the module. Enjoy!

1. *it's versus its*.

Loads and – I mean *shedloads* – of people screw this up so I'm putting it at the top of our list.

The first part of the rule is that *it's* is the short way of writing *it is*. There's nothing else it can be. So, *the screen is broken* shortens to *it's broken*.

The second part of the rule is that *its* indicates possession. People get it wrong because they expect to use an apostrophe, like in the phrase *the computer's screen is fixed.* But you can't do that, because you've already used the apostrophe in the first part of the rule. Our example becomes *its screen is fixed.*

I'm not a big fan of teaching via mistakes, but in this case I'll hammer the point home by showing you what the wrong examples look like.

WRONG – its raining today

WRONG – it's golf course was destroyed by the rain

(I'm not offering any guarantees here, but both these grammatical mistakes were picked up by Microsoft Word. But, jeez, do I miss that paperclip cartoon that used to appear.)

For a supposedly dry subject, grammar has spawned many jokes (if we're using the very widest definition of *joke*). Here's one I promised earlier:

How do you turn a duck into a soul singer?

RIGHT – fry it in a pan until it's Bill Withers

RIGHT – fry it in a pan until its bill withers

Thank you, I'm here all week.

2. *The difference between that and which.*

We all mix these up when we're speaking, but nobody really notices. The distinction between them is a fine one, and only a pedant will tell you off for confusing them at the end of a long night in the pub. In your writing, however, it's good to show that you know the difference.

As we're in a boozy frame of mind, let's start with the line *I like pubs.* I want to add some more detail to this rather bald assertion. If the new information is essential it needs to be introduced with *that.* Let me enlarge on my first statement and turn it into *I like pubs that sell beer from microbreweries.* The sentence has become more exact, changing *I like all pubs* to *I like a certain type of pub.*

We use *which* when the new information isn't vital. Let's add some further information to the enlarged example so it reads *I like the Lifeboat, which is in Margate old town, because it sells beer from microbreweries.*

Can you see why we've switched to *which?* The location of the pub is nice to know but it's not a vital part of my main sentence.

Reading out loud has always helped me choose between *that* and *which.* If there's a natural pause before the new information comes, you need a comma and *which.* If there's no pause, choose *that.*

punctuation marks you out

I love the way language has been changed by texting and tweets. Only a fool suggests you use more semi-colons in your Facebook posts of last Saturday's gig. But language has a context. Poor grammar on your CV/resume is like turning up for that vital interview at the law firm in trainers.

You can use a colon (:) to introduce a list of bullet points if you so desire. Colons are also good when a sentence introduces an example, large quotation or explanation. Take a look again at Bill Withers in 41 to see how the colon helps you 'jump' into the joke.

Aside from that, avoid colons and semi-colons (;) in business writing. They do have a place in creative writing, but look how awkward they are in this job ad from Linkedin:

> At Partnership, we see retirement differently; there is a simple belief at the heart of our business:

people with health and lifestyle issues deserve a better deal.

If a sentence appears to long for you, split it into two with a comma or a full stop. Try reading the job advert aloud to see where the punctuation should be.

We use commas in three main ways:

1. To indicate where we would pause in speech

This quarter has been extremely difficult, largely because asset prices have fluctuated considerably.

2. To separate items in a list

Short-term assets include cash at the bank, prepayments and receivables

3. To add extra information in a sentence (this is like using brackets).

Long-term liabilities, such as the new bonds issued in Q3, have taken gearing above the level agreed in the covenant.

The extra comma is a weird mistake that's becoming increasingly common. Take a simple sentence:

The operations team has downloaded the PDF

The grammatical parts here are subject (the team), verb

(what the team does) and the object (the 'what' of the sentence). Let's see what happens when we pack the subject, verb and object with extra business yawny-yawn words.

The leading edge operations team have proactively downloaded the value-enhancing PDF deliverable.

Can you see that once you cut through all this verbiage that there's still the traditional subject, verb, object structure to the sentence? But because it's such a wordy mess, some business writers are tempted to add a comma between the subject and the verb.

WRONG *The leading edge operations team, have proactively downloaded the value-enhancing PDF deliverable.*

Never do this. The subject and the verb are linked and should never be separated by a comma. Far better to cut some words than get the punctuation wrong.

part five

words

42

take me down to paradigm city

You can always tell a bad writer by their choice of words. Poor business writers find comfort in long words, believing they make them sound more credible. They don't. No one likes you more because you've written *utilise* instead of *use* or you've changed *guidelines* to *robust accountability structures*.

If your writing is rife with business jargon, you're in danger of slipping into business speak. You'll come over as a mission statement rather than a human being. Take this extract, from a press release outlining an organisation's *core initiatives* listed in their *strategic plan.*

This involves fully embedding the new judgment based, forward-looking model and actively seeking synergies.

I'm none the wiser. This has comes from the press office, remember, staffed with full-time professional communicators. Watch out for these clunky phrases when you edit your work. They make your style leaden and dull and, worst of all, they hide your personality.

good jargon, bad jargon

People start using jargon – a word or phrase that belongs to their industry – with the best of intentions. Good jargon speeds up communication between one expert and another. A report on trends in the pharmaceutical industry, for example, might contain a chapter called *The Nocebo Effect,* and most people reading it will recognise the word. Relatively few people outside of the industry will know what a *nocebo* is, and that's absolutely fine.[6]

But jargon stops working when it jumps into the wider world. Consider the word *equity*, which has distinct meanings for different professions:

1. Actor – the name of our union in the UK

---

6 The nocebo effect proves the brain's amazing power to be negative. Subjects in drug trials often report negative side effects, even when they have been given a harmless placebo. That's nocebo in action.

2. Banker – the difference between the market value of a house and its mortgage

3. Lawyer – the principle of fairness

4. Accountant – the shareholders' funds invested and retained in a company

Picture a lawyer talking to his actor friend about the funds tied up in his house and you'll immediately see what can go wrong. A buzzword that started life as precise and original will circulate quickly around the department, across the entire firm and then into the whole business world.

Later on – and more problematically – it will jump into the wider community as well. Jargon jars as soon as it leaves the group, confusing more than it enlightens. If you write to someone offering a *holistic solution,* they'll think the words are meaningless and that you are unoriginal. You can't convince people by copying clichés. They'll tune you out.

Another huge problem with business jargon is that people pretend to understand it when they don't. One phrase that confused me when I first read it was *low-hanging fruit*. I assumed the phrase referred to deals that were both easy to win and profitable. They sounded great! However, other readers interpreted *low-hanging fruit* as something rotten and unappealing.

I've never really got to clear up this dilemma, so I don't use the phrase myself and tend to nod and smile when someone describes a client – or even a person – as *low-hanging fruit.* I'd certainly never use it in my writing.

Business buzzwords stop you thinking. I once worked with a woman in the equity research department of a bank in London. She'd heard the phrase *executive decision* and really loved the adjective. She'd email to say that she'll be back late from her *executive lunch* and so would miss our *executive meeting* (looking back, that meeting she probably called it an *executive quality circle*). In her mind, using the word made her sound more professional. Not one of her colleagues shared this opinion.

If you use jargon phrases once they've lost their currency, your writing will come across as dated. What was once original can age very quickly, especially now that the net has revved up the speed of transmission.

I met a CEO during an emergency meeting for a company on its last legs – the board was desperately scrabbling around for ways to avoid insolvency and looking for inspiration.

But the CEO's presentation to the board was stuffed full of *business process re-engineering* and *just-in-time client-server logistical solutions*. These phrases were old-fashioned in 1995 and highlighted that the poor chap had even less idea about the subject matter and the potential solutions to the crisis than his audience. One of the fellow directors whispered to me 'who is this walking thesaurus of business bullshit?'

By a weird twist of fate, the same CEO sent a proposal to one of my clients nine years later. They filed it straight in the bin. Where before his phrases had merely sounded odd – *value added*, *binary approach, take possession of the problem* – he now came across like someone speaking a dying, archaic language. Don't fall into the same trap.

Jargon may deliberately be used to hide a lack of knowledge and to baffle the reader. Many of us have bluffed our way through business conversations with phrases like *I'll come back to you on that*. But that's not an option in writing. Bad jargon destroys your relationship with the reader.

when jargon jumps

Whilst killing time recently at my dentist I read a tattered lifestyle magazine from 2003 (they're pretty cutting edge at my dentist). Tacked on to the end of an article about Portland being the next Silicon Valley was a list of internet buzzwords. Many of these have disappeared (*knowledge management system, client/server interface* and *blogosphere*) but some are now part of everyday life (*webinar, podcast* and *SEO).*

Certain buzzwords 'jump' from the business world and become completely accepted. Every time you say *I'll google that* you're using a business buzzword that's become accepted currency. A similar thing is happening to *big data.* But the wider public is always scornful of business readers who use buzzwords that haven't yet jumped, so be careful with phrases like *snackable content* and the toe-curling *thought leader.*

I don't believe all jargon is bad, but I get concerned

when it jumps from a team of experts to a wider readership. If your reader doesn't know the jargon you've got two choices.

1. Replace it with vocabulary appropriate for the audience. A *bond* could be called a *tradable debt product* or an *IOU* depending on their level of knowledge.

2. Add a 'translation' in brackets, a footnote or even a glossary. This gives you more space for details without breaking up the flow of your writing. So now *bond* is explained as *a debt issued by a company or government which pays a coupon and whose repayment is guaranteed by contract on maturity.*

business 'euphemisms'

I once worked for an organisation whose leadership was big on business euphemisms. After one particular directors' meeting, a notice was posted in the staff canteen. The workforce, at the time largely made up of angry skinheads, mouthed the poster's words as they read them. The company had made *successive negative profit* so *employability resources* needed to be *right-sized*.

I watched the puzzled faces of my colleagues attempting to translate these euphemisms. Was this good news or bad? What did *termination and cessation of employee privilege* actually mean? The euphemisms were essentially a way of avoiding *sensitive subjects* (which is another euphemism, by the way). Euphemisms, typically, are about death and sex. That's why we have so many words for these subjects, many of which I heard as the employees slowly digested the bad news.

Euphemisms aren't needed in business. They create an unhealthy distance between you and your readers. What we want in moments of crisis are leaders who take responsibility and explain in clear language. Better to call something a *disaster* rather than an *incident*. If you skirt around the subject, people won't understand you and they certainly won't trust you.

the gist, not the quintessence

I'll make no bones about it. I loved the word *quintessence*. I felt really intelligent whenever I used it. I was exultant for my readers! How lucky they were to read the thoughts of a man who had done so well in his Latin exams.

But it slowly dawned on me that a word like *quintessence* creates problems. Firstly, it made me sound pompous, which – and this may surprise you – had never been one of my aims. It also took up a lot of space on the page. And many people didn't know what it meant.

For every word in English with a Latin root, there's an Anglo-Saxon alternative. The Anglo-Saxon is normally one or two syllables long, so it's shorter and more popular with your readers. The more you go Anglo-Saxon rather than Latin, the punchier your writing will be.

There's no difference in meaning between *the client relationship has ended* and *the client relationship has terminated*. But *end* is more human than *terminated*, and writing like a person rather than a committee will definitely get you more readers.

I learned my lesson with *quintessence* and now use *gist* instead.

Here's a list of the most common Latin words you read in business writing. Translate them into Anglo-Saxon to connect with your readers.

Avoid	Use
Adjacent	Next to
Administer	Give
Alleviate	Ease
Approximately	About
Assistance	Help
Commencement	Start
Demonstrate	Show
Discontinue	End
Endeavour	Try
Facilitate	Help
Identical	Same
Inform	Tell

Avoid	Use
Initiate	Start
Magnitude	Size
Necessitate	Need
Parameter	Limit
Particulars	Details
Prohibit	Ban, Stop
Purchase	Buy
Receive	Get
Regulation	Rule
Request	Ask
Requirement	Need, Want
Terminate	End

kick out the yawns

Certain words and phrases are terribly overused in business writing and have little meaning. These are what I call Yawny-Yawns. I know that's not a precise term but it's better than calling them *obfuscatory circumlocutions*, is it not?

These are the *ums* and *ahs* of writing, the pauses where a writer tries to collect their thoughts. My early drafts of work often contain these words because I've not yet clarified my ideas. Once I get to the editing stage I cut them out. You must do the same.

figure 38 Herewith, some yawny words

Avoid	Use
At a later date	Later
At this moment in time	Now
For the purpose of	For, To
In addition to	Also
In relation to	About
On a regular basis	Often

Do a search in your current document for these phrases, and replace them with the alternative. Your word count will go down and your readability will increase.

let's leave legal language to the lawyers

There's a place for legal language. It's in legal documents. Legal vocabulary belongs in dusty courts and dry-as-dust contracts. It's perfect when precise distinctions have to be made.

But words like *heretofore* and *aforementioned* don't belong in your day-to-day business writing. People slip these in because they think it makes them sound impressive and learned. They don't. Using legal words in your emails makes you sound as weird as a man in a pub proclaiming *herewith a round of drinks*.

Here's a list of legal-sounding words that you need to excise forthwith from your writing:

figure 39 Hencetofore, ditch the legal language

Avoid	Use
At the present time	Now
In advance of	Before
In order to	To
In the event that	If
Monies	Money
Regarding	About
Therefore	So
Thus	So

the short words club

As a service to you and your readers, here's a list of words and phrases that always make readers switch off. These are words I've collected over the years giving feedback on pitch documents, stock exchange reports, book proposals and weighty manuscripts.

Avoid	Use
Accordingly	So
At a later date	Later
At this moment in time	Now
Consequently	So
For the purpose of	To, For
Frequently	Often
In addition to	Also
In order to	To
In relation to	About
On a regular basis	Often
Prior to	Before

Incidentally, these are words that are common in school and university essays. I think many people hang on to these words when they write for business. But what worked in exams and assessments doesn't necessarily work for emails and reports. Let's face facts. You might have had great teachers at school but very few of them ever worked in the world of business. Essays and school reports show a teacher that you have digested – and can reproduce – what you've learnt. Business writing is different. It's about influencing readers, rather than demonstrating your knowledge. Forget this at your peril!

The Local Government Association in Great Britain compiled a list of one hundred words that put up a barrier between the councils and the people they serve. I've taken the list and split into three categories – business buzzwords, distancing words and yawny-yawns. I've also supplied far better alternatives for you to use.

Many *business buzzwords* jump into government slang, where they join some of the ugliest words ever coined. Stripped out from their brochures and memorandum, these words appear even more ridiculous. Here are just four of the worst examples:

Avoid	Use
Beacon	Good example
Cascading	Giving, sharing
Champion	Best
Symposium	Meeting

Distancing words are depressing rather than impressive. It's possible that the policy wonk opposite you will understand – and perhaps even like – your vocabulary. But poor Joe Public, trying to work out what day to put out the recycling bins, won't be impressed by these cold, impersonal words.

Avoid	Use
Customer	Person
Spending priority	Person's need
Engagement	Talking with people
Seed bed	Idea

Many of these terms begin in central government, where they speed up communication. A phrase such as *best practice* contains a huge amount of meaning for a government profession. It describes an approach to planning, measuring and monitoring council spending to ensure that taxpayers' money is spent in an efficient and responsible manner. But when it jumps into everyday use it becomes a clumsy way of saying *being good at your job*.

Using specialised terms in business is not a sin. In fact, I prefer my dentist to say *occlusal surface* instead of *chewing bit of your fangs.* But pompous Latinate words don't magically make you a subject matter expert. Here, in a sub-category of one of my least favourite word groups, are some local government yawny-yawns. Enjoy!

Avoid	Use
Coterminosity[7]	Agreement
Facilitate	Help
Fully consensual	Complete agreement
Funding stream	Money

If you excuse an unpleasant analogy, business words are like fleas that jump from a confined area (a policy document, say, or an internal briefing) to the wider world. Which makes a bad writer, of course, the flea-bitten dog who's *cascading* these pests from their *pathfinding symposia* into the normal world.

---

7 I had to look this up, believe me.

part six

happy endings

every diamond needs a polish

The best writing comes from reviewing. Nobody gets anything of worth right first time. It's impossible. The smartest advice I ever received from a novelist – no names, no pack drill, Mr B – was to splurge out your words as quickly as you can. Then, using all the time you've saved by writing quickly, revise your drafts until they're wonderful.

Meet Francisco, a trained engineer who writes detailed manuals about household safety. Interestingly, he uses the word *produce* rather than *write.* He divides the production of his manuals into four distinct processes:

1. *Content generation.* Francisco is always looking for new writing tasks. Sometimes he generates his own ideas to pitch to his publisher. Other times he attends brainstorming meetings with his agent.[8]

---

8   Francisco hates – and I mean *absolutely hates* – the word 'brainstorm'

On occasions, a manufacturer of kettles or strip-lighting will approach him with the job.

2. *Planning and organisation.* Francisco jokes that the closest he gets to author software is Excel. He's the king of spreadsheets and mindmaps, and loves to have his ideas well-organised. His plans are immensely detailed, and he won't write a word until he knows every paragraph in his pyramid.

3. *Prototype.* Francisco produces his first draft as quickly as possible. He always begins by listing the three best ways to avoid serious problems with the product. Francisco's the guy who tells you not to rest your new aluminium ladder against the electricity pylon. His attitude is one of experimentation rather than perfection. He doesn't see this stage as creative. Rather, he's filling in the blanks left in his plan.

4. *Revision.* Given his background in manufacturing, Francisco regards quality control as vital. He spends more time tightening up his grammar and polishing his examples than he does on the writing.

Before beginning any review I return to my original objectives. Why did I decide to write? If I've not fulfilled this aim, then tinkering with split infinitives is irrelevant. I judge myself on two criteria – content and structure.

Have I written enough *content* to do the job? Is there too much, or not enough? I'm keen on planning, and I keep all of my sketchy notes, mindmaps and outlines until I'm sure the project is finished. I return to my Reader Response Model and check the FAB. I look for ways to make my writing more useful, more interesting and – this is the key during review – more enjoyable. You should do the same.

Scan your work to test your *structure*. Ignore the words you're lovingly created and instead concentrate on the section titles, chapter headings and various types of sub-header. Remember what we said about guiding your reader to the gold? The reader must be able to get the gist of your report by thumbing through it. Put yourself in their shoes and travel through the document. If you need more guidance, add more signposts *before* changing any of the text.

the reviewing mindset

Successful reviewing demands a change in mindset. You have to accept that the current version of your document is only a first draft, and that first drafts are clogged with errors and poor choices. No matter how much time, love and labour you've put in, what you have is a demo version and not the finished album.

Many writers press the send button too early. Eager to share – or anxious to tick off an item on their To Do list – they publish without reviewing their writing. This is always a mistake, because an extra 5% of effort in editing can be the difference between a successful writer and an also-ran.

Why does reviewing improve your writing? Your style will be better because you'll tighten up words, sentences and paragraphs. Your message will be clearer because you focus on influencing your reader.

You're not at school any longer, so no-one buys your

excuse about rushing because you've run out of time. Readers won't forgive your sloppiness, no matter how tight your deadline. You have to budget for revision in your planning. For me, a rough breakdown of a typical project is:

figure 40 Who knows where the time goes?

Planning	30%
Writing	40%
Revising	28%
Faffing	2%

Readers do judge writers by their errors. Don't believe me? Take a look at this picture, which belongs firmly in the category marked *you had one job to do and you still screwed it up.* How much do you trust this particular writer?

figure 41

Don't risk your reputation by sending out a first draft of anything. As a minimum, a read-through should catch missed words and poor grammar. As we come towards the end of *Smack* you'll know that business writing is much more about craft than inspiration. Reviewing is hard work, and demands patience, but it's essential. It's also your last chance to make sure that the piece is about *you the reader* rather than *me the writer.*

reviewing to cut down and re-focus

No-one will ever ask you to make your sentences longer and more convoluted. Use the reviewing time to cut down bizspeak, throw out unnecessary verbiage and sharpen up sentences.

I have a very systematic approach to reviewing. The first step is to mark the end of writing by taking a break. If I've been working at home, I'll go out to the cinema or theatre. If I'm in an office, I'll do another job for a day or so. I'm telling my brain there's a difference between the writing (which is finished for the moment) and the reviewing stage (which has yet to start).

It's so easy to lose sight of our objectives as we write. Use the review stage to remind yourself *why* you started and *what* you wanted to influence. Is the purpose of your document absolutely clear from the very first word and does the main recommendation hit the reader between the eyes? Is the structure logical and controlled? Do the examples work? If you answer *no* to any of these questions, you need to refocus.

Reviewing with honesty is often emotionally fraught. It's easy to lose confidence as you read your work, so remind yourself that readers want you to succeed because we all enjoy good writing. They won't check every word with forensic attention and most readers, once they trust you, will forgive you the odd the slip. Judge your writing on whether you think it will change their FAB.

the three p's of feedback

What does a writer look like to you? Is she a sensitive maiden, sitting under a blossoming magnolia tree in a wide-brimmed hat whilst waiting for the muse to strike? Or do you see the Hemingway type, flushed with whisky and bashing out deathless prose on an ancient Olivetti typewriter?

Let me stop you there. The best business writers ignore this myth of the solitary genius and ask for help.

Many people have bad memories of writing. These can start at a very early age, when a teacher tells us our writing is illegible. We've all had our homework covered with angry red comments and thick crossing-outs. Most of us have burned the midnight oil to achieve an impossible essay deadline only to get a *see me* scribbled at the bottom of the page. Some of you may even have received a detention for writing *Rock, Rock, Clash City Rockers* in fluorescent pink and yellow over your Religious Studies notebook. Sound familiar? Just me then.

These memories tend to make us tense at the very moment when we should be receptive to improvements and suggestions. It's no wonder that even the thought of getting feedback can make us anxious. Being aware of the three P's of feedback will get you through these emotional blocks. Repeating these thoughts will help you immensely.

You've got to keep your *perspective*. Everything can be fixed. Your first draft hasn't been carved in stone, so the odd delete or change is hardly the end of the world. Most of your work is still good.

High quality feedback is not *personal*. Most people will suggest changes that are easy to implement. You've designed and built a dream home, and they think the bathroom should be painted sky blue rather than taupe. That's not a big deal. Asking you for more details and pointing out a couple of clunky sentences does not constitute a personal attack.

It's important to remain *positive*. Instead of being petrified that someone is about to criticize, tell yourself they're helping you to be a better writer. We all make errors in our early drafts, and what they're doing will stop us from repeating those errors in public. That's a fantastic thing for them to offer. I'm not saying you have to kiss and hug them, but I do think you should view them as helpers and not enemies.

We're friends now, right? You've come so far with me in this book that I want to share my own feelings on receiving feedback. I've asked for feedback on books, reports, articles, presentations and even, on one horrific occasion, a sonnet about a M&A deal. I always work through feedback at home, never in the office. I've realised over the decades that my emotional response splits into three distinct stages.

I begin the *early stage* by thanking the kind soul for their feedback. I do this before I've even looked at it. I tell them that I'm tremendously appreciative of the time and effort they've spent on my behalf. Then I dive in, and often get angry at the stupid mistakes I've made. You know the ones – confusing *affect* ('to change') with *effect* ('a reaction to a cause'), or not noticing that the spell-checker has changed *Mississippi* to *Miss Hippie*.

I often do something to turn down my frustration level. The kettle will go on and I'll have a moody moment with Nick Cave. I score some easy wins by correcting sloppy sentences and splitting up wordy paragraphs. Loads of improvements can be made quickly and without too much effort. These tweaks immediately improve my work, but I can only make them because a second pair of eyes has pointed them out.

The *middle stage* is where hard work occurs. Feedback here includes suggestions like *move section four to the end* and *the evidence in section three is skimpy*. The middle stage is where I do significant rewrites and sometimes come up with completely new sections. It's tough, but the mood lightens because I feel better about my work (and my abilities as a writer). I'll dance around the office to some Northern Soul.

The *final stage* is always satisfying. I know the extra effort will improve my work tremendously. It's a big gain for a relatively small amount of pain. I finish by checking my changes, because sometimes a single extra word on the contents page can ruin the entire format of a document. By way of celebration, I change out of my pyjamas.

I now call the person who's given me feedback and thank them again. I'm aware they might be worried about how I've reacted to their feedback, so it's always a smart idea to let them know all is well. After that, I get ready to press send.

But you shouldn't do that until you've read the next two chapters.

feedback to use, feedback to bin

Don't assume that all feedback is equally important. There are two types of feedback that are dangerous to every writer.

The first one is the completely *complimentary*. Be wary of anyone who says *don't change anything – it's fantastic.* It may be that they lack the skill and experience needed to improve your work. Or, much more worryingly, they haven't even looked at your work and are just trying to fob you off. Completely complimentary feedback – though it makes you feel warm and happy inside – has to be ditched.

Entirely *destructive* feedback should also be given short shrift. If a boss says you should *change every single word* you face a number of what business euphemists would probably call 'interesting challenges'. On rare occasions, your boss will be both an expert on the subject matter and a brilliant writer. In the unlikely event that this is case, bite the bullet and bow down to their superior skill and knowledge. But it's my experience that people who possess these laudable attributes rarely feel the need to attack the work of others. Destructive criticism says far more about the giver than their target. Ask them for constructive advice on how to improve your work rather than a dismissal of your efforts.

You've got to identify the two flavours of constructive criticism if you want to be a better writer. *Suggestive feedback* is given when your work is good enough to be sent out, but could be improved – next time – with some polishing. I often feel suggestive feedback is more of a compliment than complimentary feedback. The person reading it believes your work is good enough to be made even better. Don't ignore suggestive feedback. The person giving it wants you to aim higher.

While suggestive feedback can be implemented later, *advisory feedback* must be acted upon immediately. You don't have any power of discretion when an experienced reviewer tells you *make this better by having more pull quotes and shorter paragraphs*.

Constructive criticism provides the gloss to turns something that's good enough into something really wonderful. Advice and specific tips to improve the quality of your work are especially useful if they come from people who are held in high regard by others in your department or company. Compliments are fantastic to receive but they don't improve the quality of your work. Everything is improvable, even the word *improvable*.

how to use the four main types of feedback

You have a duty to make the best use of your feedback. Don't ask someone to check your words and then not act on their suggestions.

figure 42   The Four Categories of Feedback

Complimentary	›	Suggestive	›	Advisory	›	Destructive
Don't change a thing		Perhaps next time you can change...		Make this better by changing...		Change all of it
I love you		It's good enough, but next time it can be better		It's good, but not yet good enough		You are an idiot and I am filled with self-hate

Most business writers are unaware that they can have three responses to any feedback.

The *practical response* is entirely about the short term. What will help you improve your current piece of writing and what can be put on the backburner until the deadline has passed?

The *learning response* is concerned with long-term improvement. For example, the comment *you tend to use a lot of passives* is valuable because it will steer you towards writing more active sentences in the future. These comments tell us a surprising amount about our strengths and weaknesses.

You've got to be honest with yourself when considering your *emotional response* to the feedback. Are you truly open to suggestions or are you resistant to sound advice?

Let's revisit the four types of feedback – advisory, suggestive, complimentary and destructive. What responses should they produce?

Advisory feedback creates both a practical and a learning response. It will make you change your current piece and have a long-term impact on your writing.

Suggestive feedback creates a learning response but not necessarily a practical response in the short term. There's no obligation to change your current piece, but the spirit of suggestive feedback is to change your writing over the longer term.

Neither *complimentary* nor *destructive* feedback should

lead to a practical response. They are both *unreliable witnesses*. But both will provoke emotional responses – one overly positive, the other overly negative – that you must recognise if you are to control them.

figure 43 **Responses to the Four Categories of Feedback**

Complimentary
Practical - No
Learning - No
Emotional - Yes

Suggestive
Practical - No
Learning - Yes
Emotional - No

Advisory
Practical - Yes
Learning - Yes
Emotional - No

Destructive
Practical - No
Learning - No
Emotional - Yes

how to give feedback without getting punched

You'd tell your colleague if they had egg stains on their tie or were – ahem – unzipped after a visit to the bathroom. You're doing the same with feedback, but with their writing rather than their clothes.

Our excuses for not giving feedback split into the practical and the emotional. We know that reviewing a colleague's writing is going to take *time*. We're all pushed for time at work and making suggestions is a commitment that can't be done in a slapdash fashion. Who can blame us for avoiding yet another commitment?

Sometimes we don't want to give feedback because we don't want to *upset friends.* We run the risk that they'll take our comments as personal criticism. After all, we reason, destructive criticism of our own work has hurt *our* emotions in the past. We all recognise that flash of pain across someone's face when they've been criticised. But it's better to tell them that spellchecker has changed *the pen is mightier than the sword* to *the penis mightier than the sword* before the first run of a million books goes to print.

We're also wary of criticising those above us in the *work hierarchy*. I worked with one of the descendants of the Cooper Brothers. We occasionally thawed him out to give presentations to the stuffier clients. I used to edit his pitch packs, and noticed that he always wrote *pacifically* when he meant *specifically*. I also know that he never listened to me, no matter how many degrees in English I'd managed to plunder. I'm using *Smack* to finally confess that, even though I changed his error on many occasions, I never told him. I saw little upside in antagonising someone who could sack me.

We may believe that we *lack sufficient knowledge* to give credible feedback. We ask ourselves, what on earth do I know about agricultural spending trends or pop-up operating theatres? But you've not been asked to give feedback primarily on their content. What colleagues want are your opinions on word choice, sentence construction and presentation.

figure 44   Why You Don't Like Giving Feedback

how to boost the quality of your feedback

I've got two practical tips that have worked wonders.

Under the *buddy system* you find a colleague whose writing you admire. Don't choose a close friend because they won't be harsh enough on your work when it's most needed. Strike a deal with them. Agree to swap feedback on the same amount of work. It could be, say, three pieces a month, or ten improvements per piece.

You can develop even further by getting *feedback on your feedback*. I know this sounds a bit New Age, but it's actually a great way to better writing and improved self-awareness. You don't need a huge discussion with your buddy. It's enough to spend five minutes on what's good about the feedback and what didn't work.

Both these techniques strengthen the bond between you and your reviewer. The trust you share will produce even higher quality feedback in the future. It's likely that your feedback buddy will start the process with exactly the same fears and worries you've just read about. By the time you've worked with them a few times, you'll accept their constructive feedback with grace. You'll even – gasp – look forward to receiving it.

I've swapped work with a friend in LA for years. Sean and I have developed our own personal code for rapid communication. FOF means *file in the fire* and LOG means *load of garbage. NME* is our code for *need more examples* and SHIT translates as *a little more work is needed to reach your true potential.*

the difference between reviewing and proofing

You may believe that the fat lady is doing her vocal warm-ups, but you're still a way from being finished. Proofing is your last chance to correct errors and catch mistakes, and takes place after you've worked on your feedback.

Proofing is only worthwhile if your text has already been polished. You're no longer the sculptor, but the guy with the broom who makes sure the studio is neat and tidy.

Professional proof readers aren't normally the most talkative of people, but my friend Lesley, who proofs etymological dictionaries, gave me some good tips during her lunch break at Oxford University Press. Her first suggestion was simply brilliant. Before you take a scalpel to your work, make sure you email yourself a copy. If you really screw up the edits – and that's entirely possible – at least you have an original safe and sound in cyberspace.

Proofing is a strain on the eyes, so watch out for tiredness. Lesley recommends staring out the window and doing nothing for five minutes every thirty minutes or so (some of you may already have perfected this technique).

Focus on the areas of maximum risk. Headlines, place names and numbers in lists are all repeat offenders. Check peoples' names at least three times. Even more, if they have a glamorous surname like Loizou.

Errors tend to appear in clusters. This happens because you were exhausted, distracted or unsure of your content when you were writing. If you spot one mistake, there's often another lurking close by.

In an ideal world, you'd have a proof reader at your shoulder. This is rarely the case so, once more, a change in mindset is needed. You have to deliberately strip off your writer's cardigan and put on your editor's hat.

I once sent out an email which contained the line *all of us are bland to our own mistakes.* Most people thought it was me trying to be clever and/or funny. It wasn't. It was a stupid error that I didn't spot because we are blind to our own mistakes, aren't we? Spell-checkers are great, but they don't catch this type of error and are a bit random with grammar.

What to do? Get a printout. Professional proofers place a ruler under the line to force them to concentrate on the text. They point to each word with their finger or a pen as they read. Most of us in the 21st century don't keep a ruler handy, but any straight edge will do. Anything that boosts your focus will work. I print out lengthy emails and reports, but proof short emails by tapping a pen on each word on the screen. Sounds nerdy, but it's effective.

My review begins with a *hitlist*. These are the writing 'mannerisms' that infest my first drafts. All of us are different, but here are the things I always change during my first review:

1. Academic style – I enjoyed school and university, and I sometimes slip back into lengthy paragraphs and complex footnotes

2. Make and made – I use these superfluous verbs too much

3. Lack of sentence variation – I write too many short sentences, so run the risk of creating a monotonous rhythm

4. Words I overuse – I keep a sharp eye out for *very* (which is rarely needed), *always* (which is rarely true and makes me sound narrow-minded) and *just* (as in *just a bit*)

5. My favourite word is *erudite.* I have never used this word in business writing.

Reducing your word count helps your reader find your subject. Weak paragraph construction and flabby construction hide your meaning. Don't make your reader hack through your writing with a machete.

But be aware that too much pruning can also be harmful. Resist the temptation to delete paragraphs that you now think are too basic. The majority of your readers are *not* experts in your field. They want you to explain concepts and give examples. You need to score the easy marks to pass any exam.

Let's not get all misty-eyed for a golden age of editing and reviewing. It's clear that the internet has led to a slip in standards. Go to the websites of any major new organization – hello, the BBC! – and you'll find typos and clunky sentences. The truth is that few scanners notice, and even less care.

The internet is a content-munching monster that demands writing. Over forty quadrillion words are published every second on websites, tweets, blogs and other types of communication that hadn't even been invented at the time I made up this statistic. This is a massive opportunity for those who know how to communicate, because everybody with a computer can publish. The problem is that not everyone with a computer can write.

Hewlett Packard spends millions of dollars advertising its printers. It's a shame, then, that they didn't have a couple of hundred bucks to get a proof reader to check their copy. You know it's going to be bad writing as soon as you read the headline – *HP, the world's most preferred printers*. Strictly speaking, there's nothing wrong with the headline but it's clumsy and wordy. Did they mean *favourite*?

Asking a question is normally a great way to get the reader's attention. But leaving out the question mark is a great way to make readers really sceptical about the quality of your company.

When there is so much pressure on costs and efficiency in education, isn't it great to find an unexpected source of savings.

This mistake is all-the-more glaring because HP's case study is designed to sell more printers to schools. If anyone is going to be critical of your grammar mistakes, it'll be the teachers at a British grammar school. Why ruin your credibility by not getting your work checked?

There's also some terrible jargon on this page. The claim that HP understands the *criticality of security in education* may well be true, but most people won't get past the word *criticality.* And has there ever been a blander adjective than *appropriate* in the phrase *appropriate use of colour fuels the imagination and improves learning?*

There's something not quite right about the whole campaign, as if it's been designed by a disgruntled employee who's just about to quit. How else can we explain a phrase like *workgroups thrive with proactive manageability tools*? This language is fine for the Facebook group HP runs for – and I kid you not – printer fanatics. It's no good for the rest of us though.

reading aloud

The most effective way to find errors in your writing is to read it aloud. Find a quiet space and let rip. You'll feel a bit weird until you get used to it, but no finer method of proofing exists. And it's far better to feel uncomfortable in a small room than make gigantic mistakes in public (if you are genuinely worried about looking strange, tell people you are on a conference call and shut the door behind you).

Stumbling over a sentence is usually a warning that it needs a reworking. If it gets you (the writer) tongue-tied, then imagine what impact it will have on your poor reader. Stumbles normally indicate an abundance of polysyllabic turpitude. Get rid.

You'll notice your voice dropping off if you've put too many words or clauses in a sentence. Delete any sections that you can't be bothered to read out. Your readers won't notice they've gone. But if you hear the chop-chop-chop of too many short sentences, combine them.

Reading aloud will also identify one of business writing's biggest curses – too many words which sound similar. Listen out for horrors like *the evolution of the revolution,* and take care with *corralling the emerging* and their ilk. You'll also hear if you've repeated the same same word.

This process is far easier with a printout than on the screen. A printout will help you complete those little jobs that no-one likes doing, such as checking you've put the right references on captions and lists are correctly numbered. People screw up these steps with surprising regularity.

canny computing tips

Wow, computers, look at the way they've created soooo much leisure time for all of us. Apologies if I'm a little late on the bus with the following ideas, but here are some tips you've probably not come across.

One program I can recommend for regular writers is *Scrivener*. It's great for structuring reports and keeping research in order. It does take time to learn how to use its more advanced functions, but I've found the investment worthwhile. If you're self-editing, it's great for that *I've written a great section but don't know where it goes* feeling.

Moving paragraphs in *Microsoft Word* is easier than you think. Click three times anywhere in the paragraph to select it in its entirety. I know, it's like magic.

Stuck for the right word? *Microsoft Word* has a built in *thesaurus*, which you access either through the Tools menu or by right-clicking on the word and selecting

Synonyms. It's a bit basic, and takes away the fun of discovering new words. Far better to spend the price of half-a-cup of coffee in a second-hand bookshop to buy a *Roget's Thesaurus*.

And just so you can shut up the pub bore – the other word for a thesaurus is *onomasticon*.

Word!

where to now?

You and I have busted some myths throughout these chapters. You're now aware that writing is a skill you can learn, not a gift a handful of people are born with. Difficult subjects don't have to lead to dense, complicated writing. No-one is impressed by long paragraphs jammed full of technical words.

Smack is your starting point in business writing, not your final destination. I recommend you raise your hand every time someone needs a writer. Practice boosts your flow. The more writing you do – and the more challenges you accept – the better your writing will be.

Search for examples of good business writing and learn from them. Keep your standards high and don't put your precious name to anything that is rushed or shoddy. Get as much feedback as you can. Try your best to enjoy your writing.

I recommend you read articles in your favourite magazines to see how a good author cuts down hours of interviews into precise quotes. You'll also heighten your awareness of punctuation. Not everything that's published is perfect, so learn from clumsy sentences and weak explanations.

And, above all else, remember your reader. Thank them for their time, energy and – if appropriate – their hard-earned cash. Without them to read your words, your writing doesn't exist.

Until the next book....

Author photo by Jason Pay

one hundred and twenty-five words about the author

Andreas delivers courses in writing and finance around the world. His clients include the Bank of England, the London Stock Exchange and Lloyds. Andreas was a director of training at FT Knowledge for eleven years and was voted Best Speaker at the Financial Times *Intro to the City Program* six years running.

His first novel, *The Devil's Deal*, was published by FT Prentice Hall. Translation rights were sold in nine territories, including China, Japan and Korea.

Andreas has a first class degree in English Literature from Leeds and a Master's from Cambridge. He's a graduate of Faber & Faber's Novel Writing Academy, qualified as a chartered accountant and worked as an equity analyst.

He splits his time between Madrid and his writing desk in Margate.

www.smackpitch.com

@looEzoo

Write Better Now!

Urbane Publications is dedicated to
developing new author voices, and publishing
fiction and non-fiction that challenges, thrills and
fascinates.

From page-turning novels to innovative
reference books, our goal is to publish what
YOU want to read.

Find out more at
urbanepublications.com